Spirit of Youth

Thanks Enda

We had a wonderful experience, all the best with the Atlantic Youth Trust

Andrew.

Dean

BRANDON

McDonagh.

thanks.

Thirty years of the
Spirit of Adventure Trust

Spirit of Youth

EDITED BY TESSA DUDER & KATE THOMPSON

EXISLE
PUBLISHING

DEDICATION

'One ship, one people'

May the ripple we leave on the water be the effect from those aboard our ship,
to reach the nation, and even the world.

First published 2003

Exisle Publishing Limited,
P.O. Box 60-490, Titirangi, Auckland 1230.
www.exisle.co.nz

ISBN 0-908988-51-6

Text design and production by Dexter Fry
Cover design by Dexter Fry
Printed in China through Colorcraft Ltd., HK

ACKNOWLEDGEMENTS

Many writers and photographers have contributed to the making of this anniversary book. The editors would like to thank all those who so generously and promptly responded to calls for stories and photographs, whether finally used in the book or not.

Special thanks must go to the following:

Spirit of Adventure Trust chairman Stephen Fisher and the Fisher family for their support of the project;

HRH Prince Edward, The Earl of Wessex for his trainee memories;

CEO John Lister, Purser Sue Janett and their staff for help with compiling records (made more difficult by the tragic loss of most of the Trust's archives in 2002) and in many and various ways;

Adrienne Welch; Ron Bird; Captain Barry Thompson; Captain Paul Leppington; John Duder; Lindley Belton; Steve Mutton at Vector Networks Limited;

The *Southland Times*; the *Gisborne Herald, New Horizons* magazine and photographer Rob Griffith. Where known, photographers have been acknowledged, but we apologise for any omissions.

Finally, the Spirit of Adventure Trust and the editors together thank Gareth St John Thomas of Exisle Publishing and publisher Ian Watt, without whose enthusiastic support this thirtieth anniversary publication would not have happened. We all believe it comprises a significant contribution to New Zealand's maritime literature, both for a local readership and for those involved in similar enterprises offshore.

Tessa Duder
Kate Thompson

Auckland, April 2003

The publishers acknowledge the generous support of the Lou and Iris Fisher Charitable Trust in the publication of this book

CONTENTS

Foreword by Stephen Fisher   8
Introduction   10
The Story in Brief: A Chronology   12

PART 1: **CHALLENGE TO YOUTH**   14

Birth of an Idea (Barry Thompson)   16
The Idea Becomes Reality (Pony More)   23
The Spirit of Square Rig (John Duder)   26
Learning Through Experience (Jim Lott)   30
Kids *Can* Do It! (Nick Hylton)   35
Changing Lives (Paul Leppington)   40
Hard Decisions (Tessa Duder)   45

PART 2: **TEAMWORK**   48

The Voyagers Club (Ron Bird)   50
Voyagers Are Special People (Mike Taylor)   52
Why the Voyagers Club Works (Adrienne Welch)   57
Voyages for Disabled Trainees (Joyce Lavender)   61
Our Volunteers (Barry Thompson)   64
Managing Change in Difficult Times (Bill McCook)   66
Looking Back (Jim Varney)   70
Into the New Millennium (John Lister)   71
The America's Cup   77
A Teacher's View (Chris Basham)   78
A Magical Day, June 1992 (Janet Watkins)   81
A Sanitary Tale (Bruce Marler)   82
Rising to the Challenge (Rona McConachy)   83
Becoming a Crew (Geoff Rowarth)   86

PART 3: **SELF-DISCOVERY**   88

Taking Risks (Gillian Breckell)   90
Spirit of Adventure (HRH The Earl of Wessex)   93
A New Start (Andrea Tomlinson)   94
A Long-Time Voyager (Jane Bethell)   96
The First Female Master (Jennifer Roberts)   98
A Family Affair (Sheila Budgen)   102
Vomitology (Tom Sawyer)   105
An Excellent Apprenticeship (Margaret Pidgeon)   107
The Best of Times . . . (Tony Cooper)   111
To Be Who You Want To Be (Annette Culpan)   115
A Life-Changing Experience (Ruth Dobson-Smith)   118
Ultimate Challenge (George Brightwell)   120
Nurturing Leadership (Bronwyn Rhynd)   121
Lasting Memories (Catherine Woodward *and* Heidi Miller)   123

Glossary   125
Appendix 1: Winners of Topsail Awards   126
Appendix 2: Winners of Topgallant Awards   126
Appendix 3: Trustees of the Spirit of Adventure Trust   127
Appendix 4: Masters of *Spirit of Adventure* and *Spirit of New Zealand*   128

FOREWORD

TO RECORD ACCURATELY three decades of history and celebrate the Spirit of Adventure Trust's thirtieth anniversary, we need first to look back at our origins.

A taste for the sea was developed by my late parents, Lou and Iris Fisher, my three sisters and me aboard the family yacht, *Imatra*, a 73-foot Brixham trawler. Here were sown the seeds of the iconic youth development organisation we know today. An integral part of my father's concept was a development programme for the trainees, eventually articulated in the Trust's stated aim 'to offer equal opportunity to young New Zealanders to develop qualities of leadership, independence and community spirit through the medium of the sea.'

Lou Fisher formed the Spirit of Adventure Trust in 1972, built and launched STS *Spirit of Adventure* in 1973 and shortly thereafter gifted the vessel to the Trust and the youth of the nation. With Captain Pony More at the helm as master and James Lennox-King as the operations director, the first voyages began early in 1974.

The Trust has reformed itself structurally to suit its expanding operations. With the advent of *Spirit of New Zealand* in 1986, the administration grew at a rapid rate and we found ourselves not only operating a youth development programme but also running a travel agency, a ships' providoring business and a mini shipyard for maintenance, refit and survey work. We had numerous committees each with a trustee in the chair, an executive council which reported the findings of the committees to the Trust Board, and an operations officer (later director) who ran the daily operation.

A major restructure at this point became inevitable. The committees and council were disbanded and the operations director's responsibilities were increased to those of chief executive officer. Overall, a professional, not-for-profit business was the result. The Trust Board was now in a position to caretake the Trust Deed, ensure the policies and aims were met and plan for the future.

Reflecting on the challenges for the youth of today against those of thirty years ago, I perceive a difference. It is no longer just the ability to perform, it is also the ability to make the right choice. To run a race or compete at any level now requires decisions on the numerous options available from the gear to use and wear (or be seen in) to nutrition, training methods, psychology and so on. Our training methods aboard the ship have also similarly evolved to equip our trainees for their future needs. The challenge remains to encourage individuality, instil discipline, provide a safe, friendly and enjoyable environment and retain a sense of adventure. Our safety record remains enviable.

To meet these challenges, the Trust continues to set appropriate policy. The executive staff manages the operation within the guidelines of those policies and the sea-going and office-based staff delivers the programme, all with great results.

The success of the programme can be judged in two ways. First, the demand for berths remains strong in today's market, with many more choices for youth development and outdoor education than when we started our operation in the early 1970s. Secondly, the completion of each voyage sees its mix of laughter and tears, and of enduring friendships forged as more confident trainees step ashore.

A day out recently on *Spirit of New Zealand* reminded me that the ship is a world unto herself and provides a great environment for the effectiveness of the programme, allowing the trainees to develop through participation and self-reliance. *Spirit* has indeed become 'one ship, one people'. Now let the story be told . . .

Stephen Fisher
Chairman, Spirit of Adventure Trust Board

INTRODUCTION

CHALLENGE TO YOUTH

FOR ANY SEA TRAVELLER, one of the great moments of the journey is arriving at a wharf and seeing a ship, your ship, for the first time – especially if she is a sailing ship! There she is, alongside the wharf, already at one with the elements of wind and water, no other exactly like her.

What promise she offers in those narrow ladders that lead upwards to sturdy wooden yards. Thick wires hold the masts upright, but the new sailor's eyes are invariably drawn to the daunting complexity of ropes. How long will it take to learn their names, what each does?

The eye then drops to the wooden deck, the lifeboats and, aft, the handsome wheel. The deckhouse, below which a number of people will eat and sleep. One challenge starts right there, on the wharf as the young trainee carries a bag across the gangplank to find, first, a numbered bunk and a minimalist locker. It may be the first time the trainee has ever left the family home.

In 1970 Auckland businessman Lou Fisher, inspired by the British notion of 'sail training' for youth, set in motion a vision that would result in a handsome two-masted staysail schooner *Spirit of Adventure* being launched in Auckland on 7 December 1973, and gifted to the youth of New Zealand.

By today's educational standards, his objective was disarmingly simple: give boys from all round the country the chance to enjoy the fabled Hauraki Gulf on a decent-sized yacht, and learn something about sailing, teamwork and themselves. Within a year girls were being included. Disabled trainees could sail too. Twelve years later, there was a second ship, with higher masts, a longer bowsprit and space for 40 trainees.

Why square rig? What is unique about the *Spirit* experience that sets it apart from other outdoor experiences available to young New Zealanders? And how can a bunch of teenagers possibly learn enough in nine days to sail the ship themselves?

In Part One, five masters write of the challenges – to youth, and indeed everyone connected with the organisation – that over thirty years have come to be better understood.

TEAMWORK

TEAM AND TEAMWORK are overworked words in the business-model world we live in today. Some would say that a square-rigged sailing ship provides the clearest opportunity in this modern age to demonstrate what happens when a team works together and when it doesn't. Teamwork learned in watches, each one competent and working in harmony with the other, is what gets a sailing ship moving majestically through the water.

A heavy mainsail cannot be raised by one person alone, especially in adverse conditions. It could conceivably be hoisted by two or three skilled in handling ropes and the use of block and tackle. Raising and lowering sail is best and most safely done by a team of five to ten, with the jobs of hauling and belaying (securing) clearly understood.

The challenge shared with all outdoor education experiences is the weather, but with a ship there is also the unforgiving and potentially hostile element of the sea. Teamwork is ideally learned when conditions are benign – light winds, smooth seas, a ship well away from land or hidden reefs.

When conditions turn nasty a team's skill and trust are put to the test. Anyone who has tried to get *Spirit of Adventure*'s upper fisherman staysail down in a squall or needed to tack *Spirit of New Zealand* away from a lee shore will know that.

Successful teamwork at sea leads to an awareness of how teams are important in ordinary life on land. This awareness has not been confined to the young or the seagoing, as some of the stories in Part Two show. Teamwork, from the Trust Board and its top management down, is what got the Trust through the 1987 share market crash and the subsequent difficult years.

Teamwork got the special voyages for the disabled up and running and was the fundamental concept behind the five-day leader manager courses and Spirit Trophy voyages. Teamwork binds together the Voyagers Club and the nationwide network of adult volunteers. And teamwork was the only way that *Spirit of New Zealand* was to be pulled off Tryphena Beach on Great Barrier Island in September 1995, the worst incident in the Trust's history.

It's an article of faith from the Trust Board down that the lessons in teamwork learned in ten intense days on one of the *Spirit* ships are being applied by ex-trainees out there in their communities, businesses, schools and family life.

SELF-DISCOVERY

TODAY'S YOUNG PEOPLE sail a charted world with little, at least on the surface, left to discover. So the *Spirit* discovery is internal and individual – of self, capacity for discipline, discomfort, laughter, stamina, compassion.

In 30 years, it has been realised that discovery is not confined to the teenage trainees for whom the scheme was established. In Part Three you will read of trainees' appreciation for what they (and others) claim was a life-changing experience and, equally, of adult crew and volunteers whose lives have been radically affected.

Families, for instance, whose trainee children led to mum and dad's long-time involvement. A young woman teacher who began as a mate on *Spirit of Adventure* and 15 years later sails as master of a container ship. A grandmother who reluctantly offered herself as cook and now climbs the mast as a volunteer mate. Early trainees who still sail 25 years later as watch officers and others who learned committee skills through serving on the Voyagers Club National Executive. A prince who acknowledges that the sea is 'a very humbling experience and survival, let alone making progress, depends on teamwork and trust.'

Social scientists have tried to measure the impact of outdoor education with only limited success. Those who believe that the *Spirit* experience can and does change lives for the better base their conviction on many years of positive feedback and a certain amount of faith. In the pages of this book you will discover why.

Tessa Duder   Kate Thompson

THE STORY IN BRIEF: A CHRONOLOGY

1970   Auckland industrialist Lou Fisher begins planning a youth training vessel, based on British models and requesting no support from government, to bring youth from all over New Zealand to sail in the Hauraki Gulf.

1972   Trust Board is set up, its mission to fundraise for and safely operate a sail-training youth development vessel. Trainees will be aged 14 to 18, chosen by their schools, and pay same rate from anywhere in New Zealand with Trust subsidising all travel. Voyages will be for ten days.

1973   8 December, *Spirit of Adventure*, a 90-foot staysail schooner able to carry 30 trainees and five crew, is launched at Westhaven in Auckland.

1974   Voyage 1, all boys, sails to Kawau and Te Kouma; in June, two yards are fitted; Voyage 11, first girls' voyage; first voyage for deaf trainees.

1975   Voyagers Club is established for ex-trainees; first weekend sailing for adult supporters as fundraising for youth voyages.

1977   Voyage 70, *Spirit of Adventure* is almost driven ashore on Mayor Island, but towed off by Tauranga Harbour Board tug; 2000th trainee; death of Lou Fisher; appointment of his son Stephen as chairman.

1978   Voyage 100, trainee berths are reduced from 27 to 25 to allow more crew space.

1979   Leading hands (ex-trainees) position is established; *Spirit of Adventure* undertakes first southern voyage to Wellington and Marlborough Sounds.

1980   *Spirit of Adventure*'s second southern voyage, south to Lyttelton.

1981   *Spirit of Adventure*'s third southern voyage, south to Bluff and Oban, Stewart Island; nearly 5000 trainees have completed ten-day voyages.

1982   *Spirit of Adventure*'s fourth southern voyage, first passage around North Cape; Trust Board launches $2m fundraising campaign for *Spirit of New Zealand*; Jennifer Roberts sails as first woman master.

1983   *Spirit of Adventure* embarks on fifth and longest southern voyage, fundraising as she goes for *Spirit of New Zealand*; tenth anniversary celebrations; keel of *Spirit of New Zealand* is laid at Henderson, Auckland.

1984   *Spirit of Adventure* completes first circumnavigation of New Zealand; first weekend for disabled trainees Voyage 241; Rolls-Royce raffle captures public imagination and raises more than $650,000 for the new ship.

1985   First four-day voyages for disabled trainees; by end of 1985, *Spirit of Adventure* has sailed around 95,300 nautical miles, with about 7330 trainees completing ten-day trips.

1986   24 February, famous Kiwi round-the-world sailor Dame Naomi James launches *Spirit of New Zealand*, 45.2 metres, three-masted brigantine able to carry 42 trainees and 12 crew. December 1986 to April 1987 she visits 14 ports around New Zealand, saying thank you.

1987   First regional association is formally launched, in Wellington.

1988   *Spirit of New Zealand* visits Melbourne, Hobart and Sydney to represent New Zealand in the 1988 Australian Bicentennial celebrations. By July nearly 10,000 trainees have passed through the Trust's ten-day programmes.

1986-1996	The Trust operates two ships, both undertaking extensive coastal voyages on ten-day, weekend, leader manager and disabled voyages, through periods of economic downturn, the stresses imposed by Tomorrow's Schools and growth of alternative opportunities for young people within the outdoor education market.
1993	Spirit of Adventure Foundation is formed to create a capital fund, separate from operating funds, for a new vessel to replace *Spirit of New Zealand* around 2015; by 2003, it has 100 life members.
1995	*Spirit of New Zealand* grounds at Tryphena Harbour on Great Barrier Island, is pulled off after four days with no structural damage or injury to trainees; operations office begins the move from Marsden Wharf to Prince's Wharf.
1997	Trust Board makes difficult decision to sell *Spirit of Adventure* to Captain Cook Cruises in Nadi, Fiji; she is decommissioned in August and sails for Fiji in November. *Spirit of New Zealand* begins new era of intensive back-to-back ten-day voyages to meet the ongoing demand for berths.
1998	The 25,000th trainee sails on Voyage 270; Trust Board institutes the Topgallant Awards (two annually) for long and distinguished service to the Trust, beginning with 11 retrospective awards; Spirit Trophy voyages begin, offering five-day voyages to 14-year-olds, and are immediately popular with schools.
1999	Major new office computer system installed; 25th jubilee celebrations of Voyagers Club; October to March 2000, *Spirit of New Zealand* undertakes programme of sailings associated with the millennium events in Gisborne and the America's Cup regatta in Auckland.
2000	*Spirit of New Zealand's* charter work during America's Cup raises $250,000 towards its youth development programme; the 15-year-old *Spirit of New Zealand* gets a half-life survey and refit, costing more than half a million dollars; operations office moves to 1 Queen Street, leaving the Bosun's Office in the portacoms on Prince's Wharf.
2001	New trainee scholarship scheme combines grant from Team New Zealand and existing J W McKenzie Trust to help disadvantaged trainees.
2002	Search for new premises intensifies; by October all hurdles have been cleared to build on Prince's Wharf, on eastern end of Maritime Museum. Nearly 50,000 trainees have sailed with the Trust since 1973.
2003	*Spirit of New Zealand*, on fundraising day charters, provides windward mark for the Louis Vuitton and America's Cup races; August, planned completion date of new Trust headquarters on Prince's Wharf; 30th anniversary celebrations, including a new book, are planned for November 2003.

PART 1

CHALLENGE TO YOUTH

BIRTH OF AN IDEA

BARRY THOMPSON

Captain Barry Thompson, on his retirement from the Spirit of Adventure Trust Board and appointment in 1998 as vice-patron, had given over 25 years' service as a founding trustee and deputy chairman, and as a regular volunteer master. He is acknowledged as the principal advocate for square rig on Spirit of Adventure and for the introduction of adult weekend voyages in 1976.

FEBRUARY 1972. I awoke early one Sunday morning and saw the golden opportunity at last for a restful lie-in — time for a cup of tea in bed and the final chapters of my book, *Impelled into Experience*, by J.M. Hogan.

It was an account of the early days of the Outward Bound movement and of Kurt Hahn's philosophies applied so successfully at the first Outward Bound School at Aberdovey in Wales. Back in 1945 I'd undergone a month's training at that remarkable school just before going to sea. I've long considered it one of the most worthwhile experiences of my life. It undoubtedly did just what it claimed — to help a lad discover himself and realise his potential.

Now, in 1972, more than 25 years later, and after many years at sea in the Merchant Service and the Royal Navy, I'd successfully developed my own business as a marine surveyor. In 1963 I 'swallowed the anchor' but continued in New Zealand's naval reserve. As a lieutenant commander, I'd recently been appointed as the executive officer of HMNZS Ngapona, headquarters of its Auckland division.

As I finished the final chapter of my book I began to muse upon the possibility of introducing some of Kurt Hahn's ideas into the training programme of our young naval reserve ratings. I was utterly convinced of their value to young people and had not long been thinking about this exciting possibility when the telephone rang.

'Lou Fisher here. Barry, you have a number of glossy English yachting magazines in your office, haven't you?

Those with photos at the back advertising large yachts for sale in the Mediterranean and elsewhere?'

'Yes, Lou, I have. Why?'

'Good. I'll be right over. I'll meet you in your office in half an hour.'

Before I had time to discuss either Lou's interest or his urgency, or my own availability, he had rung off. It was fairly typical of the man. Lou had an idea in his head and was not going to let anything slow him down. So much for my lie-in. I reluctantly put my book away and dressed, grabbed a piece of toast and drove to the office.

Lou duly arrived full of enthusiasm and impatience, greeted me and blurted, 'I want to buy a large yacht to take young people sailing in the Hauraki Gulf.'

His proposals clearly involved young people and sailing. Both interested me. He really didn't have too many clear ideas at that stage, but I liked his general thinking and his wish to give young people an opportunity for adventure on the sea.

'Sounds exciting,' I said. 'I'm very interested, Lou, as you might expect me to be, given my experiences at Outward Bound and years at sea.'

I don't remember whether it was then or later that Lou told me of his plan to form a Trust to operate his proposed ship, but I felt that I'd said enough to convince him of my genuine interest. He promised to keep me informed and I hoped that he might think of including me in any such venture.

After a few more words, Lou was off with the back numbers of my *Yachting World* magazines, almost as impatiently as when he had arrived and deep in thought about the possibilities and challenges presented by his

Previous page: Trainees on an early *Spirit of Adventure* voyage practising their knots.

Lou Fisher on board *Spirit of Adventure.* (Ron Bird)

new project. Were they, I wondered, just the romantic dreams of a wealthy man, or was there a real possibility that he would eventually translate them into something very worth while for a few fortunate young New Zealanders? Could this, perhaps, provide me in due course with an even better opportunity to put some of Kurt Hahn's philosophies into practice?

Who was this Lou Fisher? And how had I come to know him?

Like so many young New Zealanders, Lou spent the years 1941-45 first in the North African desert, and then fighting his way up Southern Europe throughout the Italian campaign. When the war ended Sergeant Fisher, at 34 and still single, had no reason to hurry home, choosing rather to take his demob in Britain where he hoped to make business contacts before returning to New Zealand.

One day in mid-1945, Lou walked into the London office of the Kelvinator Corporation, represented back in Auckland by his brother Woolf's firm, Fisher & Paykel. Here he met its chief engineer, Tommy Thompson. Very quickly the two men formed a firm friendship.

Tommy was a warm and friendly person who clearly found this blunt, no-nonsense Kiwi very much a man after his own heart. As a New Zealander, Lou interested him for other reasons too. I was Tommy's son, aged seventeen, had just left school and was about to become an apprentice with the Port Line, a well-respected shipping company whose ships ran regularly to Australia and New Zealand. Doubtless my ship would be calling at Auckland and no doubt father felt that Lou might keep an eye on me.

Shortly afterwards I met Lou. He came to stay with us for a couple of days and on the day of his arrival had just become engaged by telephone to an English girl he'd met recently in London. Unaware of this at the time, and of course that she would later become Mrs Iris Fisher, I must have been rather tedious, eager as I was to talk about the country I'd soon be visiting.

A little earlier, my parents allowed me to begin my own love affair with London, once the air raids had ceased shortly before the end of the war in Europe. Soon the lights went on again in a West End still full of servicemen from all the countries that had fought for the Allied cause. The city buzzed with excitement and I revelled in being there. Seventeen and about to go to sea, I intended to make the best of my time in London.

It was therefore particularly exciting when Lou unexpectedly invited me to join him there for a day or two. He'd assured my parents that young Barry would come to no harm in his care, introducing me to the London of a New Zealand soldier on demob leave.

Lou had a room in the Garrick Hotel near the bottom of Charing Cross Road and, with a mattress on the floor, I had a bed. It was most conveniently located almost opposite the New Zealand Forces Club and I well remember being taken to the club and drinking a pint or two with Lou's Kiwi friends. It's strange to look back — little did I know then that twenty-five years later I too would be a New Zealander.

Lou and Iris were married in London in September 1945 and sailed for the USA shortly afterwards. After more business contacts in America they boarded a liner in San Francisco for Auckland.

Over the next two years or so I visited Auckland about every six months. Each time Lou gave me the key of the door and made me feel at home. But by early 1949 I left Port Line and after getting my second mate's certificate I joined P & O as a junior officer. Unfortunately this meant that I would not return to New Zealand again until twelve years later, and it was to be another three before I finally settled there.

Meanwhile Lou and Iris were occasionally in London where my parents invited them aboard their 16-metre motor launch *Wayfarer* in Paris. They cruised the French canals where Lou began to enjoy a taste for small craft.

During the 1950s and 1960s Lou's interest in yachting developed further. To the great surprise of his family he announced one day in 1958 that he had bought the fine old, ketch-rigged, ex-Bristol Channel pilot cutter *Imatra* from Sir Ernest Davis. His son Stephen, his three daughters and their school friends were to spend many a happy family day afloat on this handsome 73-foot classic. On her, Lou first experienced the pleasure of taking groups of youngsters sailing in the Hauraki Gulf.

He then began thinking of another yachting project, and after that intriguing day in February 1972 when he had borrowed my English yachting magazines, Lou began to plan seriously. *Imatra* had sown the seeds in Lou's mind and now, a respected and successful businessman, he determined to buy a large second-hand and more modern yacht to give a few more young New Zealanders the experience of sailing some of the country's most beautiful coastal waters.

When nothing came of the second-hand yacht-buying venture, Lou turned to his old friend Jack Brooke and commissioned him to design a 75-foot cruising ketch for his intended purpose. The story of how Lou's idea developed into the commissioning of *Spirit of Adventure* has been well chronicled elsewhere; all I need to add is to outline how Lou's dream fitted in so well with developments in sail training overseas.

In the 1930s almost all organisations that used sailing ships for training young people did so to provide experience to those going to sea as a profession. In Britain's case, except for the use of small craft, this largely ceased for the Royal Navy around 1892, when it decided that sailing ships did not provide appropriate training for its officers and seamen in the age of steam. In the British Merchant Service this type of training lasted a little longer and was carried out in vessels employed in worldwide trading, carrying a large number of cadets who were required to play a major part in operating the ships. But they too had largely disappeared by about the time of the First World War. (Two shipping companies were prominent in this: the White Star Line and the Devitt & Moore, which later founded Pangbourne Nautical College in 1917.)

New Zealand was no stranger to sail training for its professional seamen. For several years before the First World War, the Union Steam Ship Company operated the three-masted barque *Dartford* as a commercial trading ship carrying a large number of cadets, and between 1905 and 1921 the New Zealand Government ran a former naval ship, the barquentine *Amokoura*, as a training ship based in Wellington.

Later, during the years 1941-48, many young New Zealanders gained their early sea-going experience as ordinary seamen, members of the crew of the four-masted barque *Pamir*, then operating under the New Zealand flag as a commercial trading ship. Tragically, in 1957, the *Pamir*, then under the German flag and carrying both cadets and cargo, capsized with a heavy loss of life in a North Atlantic hurricane.

Many other countries, principally in Scandinavia, Central Europe and South America, have continued to use sailing ships (often known as school ships) for the training of professional officers and seamen, even right up to the present day. The square-riggers of the Finnish shipowner, Gustav Erikson, in the years before the Second World War, carried a number of young men but, as for New Zealanders later in the *Pamir*, they were employed purely as part of a commercial venture and without any

On board Lou Fisher's gaff ketch *Imatra* in the late 1950s. Trustee John Duder is on the left and a young Stephen Fisher leaning on the rail at right. (John Duder)

real thought to their training, valuable though their experience was. Later to become a noted travel writer, the young Eric Newby wrote in *The Last Grain Race* a fascinating account of his experiences as a seaman homeward bound in Gustav Erikson's barque *Moshulu* in 1937, participating in one of the last of the pre-war grain races from Australia to Europe.

It was principally in the years between the two World Wars that the idea started to take root of using sailing ships to provide adventure and a challenge to young people not intent upon a life at sea. One notable adventurer with this in mind was Captain Alan Villiers whose diminutive square-rigger, *Joseph Conrad*, only a hundred feet in length, made a circumnavigation of the world between 1934 and 1936 manned largely by young people with a similar sense of adventure. (She is today preserved at Mystic Seaport Maritime Museum in the USA.) During the last 75 years or so others have operated small sailing craft for the purpose, but the real surge in their use followed the Second World War.

By the 1950s there was still a handful of square-riggers left afloat, mostly the school ships of the nations that continued to realise the value of professional sail training, but they were a dying breed.

Perhaps a little strangely, considering his country had long abandoned this type of sea training, it was an English lawyer, Bernard Morgan, who suggested running a tall ships race. His purpose was to bring together, possibly for the last time, these beautiful ships and their young crew, in a spirit of friendly competition and goodwill. A committee was formed, the race planned, and these ships met in Torbay in 1956 to take part in the first Tall Ships Race to Lisbon.

Other smaller sailing craft, manned largely by young people, were able to enter the race too, competing in different classes. Interestingly, this included a ketch, *English Rose II*, crewed almost entirely by young women, a concept that took a further two decades or so to reach full bloom. During the return race from Lisbon, one small, venerable British entry, the 1889 ketch *Moyana*, sank, but fortunately without loss of life.

That race, from Torbay to Lisbon, and the whole inter-national event, was a huge success with its gathering of sailing ships and young people participating in the spirit of friendly international competition. So successful was it that the original race committee, later formed into the Sail Training Association, planned another event for two years later. In due course, with a major sponsor on board, the well-known international 'Cutty Sark Tall Ship Races' came into being. At first the races were a biennial event, but today they are held annually during July and August.

The first race, and the drama of the loss of *Moyana*, spurred Britain, then still one of the world's leading maritime nations but lacking a true sail-training ship, to build a more impressive British entry. Preferably she would have at least some square rig. The topsail schooner *Sir Winston Churchill* was completed in 1966 after four years of fundraising. As Britain's entry in the next race she was at last able to give a tremendous boost to promoting the values of the youth sail-training movement in Britain.

But back to Kurt Hahn. During and after the Second World War, Hahn, a German-born refugee, was prominent in youth development in Britain. At its heart was the presentation of physical and mental challenges to young people outside the classroom. His philosophies were most successfully employed at Gordonstoun school and in the first Outward Bound school at Aberdovey where small sailing craft were used to further these aims. Not surprisingly, his philosophies also became an important part of the youth sail-training movement where the sea and sailing ships present the necessary challenges.

The decision to build *Sir Winston Churchill* came about partly because of national pride but also because it was realised that she would provide a valuable adventure opportunity for British youth. Although she was by no means the first sailing vessel to be used for this purpose, she was one of the first to be purpose-built for youth development and quickly became the focus of public attention. She proved so successful that a sister ship, *Malcolm Miller*, was built a year later and both vessels have taken part in almost all the Tall Ships races in European waters ever since.

Spirit of Adventure, **1985.** (Cliff Hawkins)

Voyage 1, January 1974. *Spirit of Adventure* is still rigged as a staysail schooner, without square sails.

In 1972 I joined the Sea Cadet Corps' small brig *Royalist* in Newcastle, England, to gain some square-rig experience. I was convinced that this was an essential for Lou's projected vessel if she was going to be the success she deserved to be.

Convincing Lou and Jack Brooke was another matter! They were concerned that setting and furling square sails aloft involved unacceptable risks. 'The rig is inherently dangerous,' they said. 'Just think about all those sailors in the old square-riggers who were lost at sea when they fell from the yards.' Besides, square-riggers were extremely inefficient compared with modern fore-and-aft-rigged yachts. No, our yacht would spend far too long beating out of the harbour to get anywhere worth while for the youngsters aboard. They wouldn't get much fun that way. Their idea was still for a modern, fast and efficient rig rather than one

they considered to be outmoded.

But I determined to keep up the pressure of my square-rig campaign. I needed allies on the Trust Board. Meanwhile I gained more experience as navigator on both *Malcolm Miller* and *Sir Winston Churchill*; in the latter for the 1997 Tall Ships Race from Aberdeen to Delfsjil in Holland.

I took every opportunity when in Europe and North America to visit some of the world's finest sail-training ships. Some years later I sailed for several voyages as second mate of the Jubilee Trust's three-masted barque *Lord Nelson*, built primarily for the physically disabled. This enabled me to observe how other sail-training organisations operated and to bring back that experience to the fledgeling Spirit of Adventure Trust.

Lou and Jack, to their credit, began to see that perhaps there was something in the idea that a sail-training ship might provide a challenge and not necessarily just a fast and exciting sailing experience. For a while they still had their reservations and understandably considered the rig to be inherently inefficient when beating to windward. The Trust Board, which Lou formed in 1972, slowly came to accept, and then really believe in, the wisdom of providing the vessel with some square sails.

For over a quarter of a century the Spirit of Adventure Trust has refined its ideas and many of the details of the way it functions. The words 'sail training' are little used today within the Trust, being replaced with 'youth development' because that, as with other similar organisations, is its principal aim. It uses the medium of the sea, and the challenges of a square-rigged sailing ship, to achieve its aims.

Today the Spirit of Adventure Trust operation has become unquestionably one of the most successful youth adventure schemes of its type in the world.

THE IDEA BECOMES REALITY

PONY MORE

Pony More began working for Lou Fisher in the early 1970s when Lou commissioned him to supervise the building of the ship that became Spirit of Adventure. *After the Spirit of Adventure Trust Board was formed in 1972, he became its employee and was responsible for fitting out the ship. Pony became the Trust's full-time sailing master in January 1973 and was master for* Spirit of Adventure's *first 21 voyages. He has sailed over a hundred ten-day voyages, covering 37,000 nautical miles in the two ships on those voyages alone, plus many more on weekend voyages.*

MY INVOLVEMENT with *Spirit of Adventure* was one of those 'right place, right time' experiences. I'd met Lou Fisher when I was working at Westhaven, and we'd struck up a friendship based on our common interest in yachting.

One evening in 1971, I was sitting at Lou's bach at Kawau Island after a day racing his yacht *Young Nick*. As we looked out over the bay, Lou remarked that he'd like to see a bigger ship anchored out there one day. I was reading a yachting magazine at the time and showed him an article featuring the British sailing ship *Sir Winston Churchill* saying, not particularly seriously, that perhaps we needed our own sail-training ship in New Zealand.

Lou leapt at the suggestion. He was never someone to do things by halves, and his decision to build *Spirit of Adventure* is a case in point.

He knew from the start that ten days was the right length of time for trainees to get most benefit from a voyage. I thought four days would be enough, but he soon proved me wrong. Lou really understood the moulding effect, that kids need that time to settle in, to gain confidence, to start proving themselves.

The design phase was a challenging one. Lou's original

Pony More and trainee on board *Spirit of Adventure*.

idea was for a 45-foot yacht with a 'crew' of 50 kids. Jack Brooke's sketches and sums soon put paid to that. Forty-five feet became 90 feet and 50 kids became 32. A ketch became a schooner and the schooner a topsail schooner. The ship had to be modern and easily handled by three crew when Lou used the vessel, as his original intention was that he would frequently sail on the ship too, in a sort of 'gentleman-owner' role.

But all credit to Jack Brooke. He stuck with the project and designed a ship that's timeless. I'm proud to say that it was my idea to add a cabin in place of the flush deck that Lou favoured, and I think that's one reason why *Spirit of Adventure* still looks modern today.

The ship's rig proved a contentious issue. At the time I thought the decision to build square rig was wrong because the ship just wasn't designed for it. She'd been designed as a performance yacht, which meant that we had to be very careful sailing her, especially with trainees on board. But I have to admit that it was definitely the right decision in the long run. Square rig gives the kids so much more to do and means that they really have to work as a team to sail the ship. If we'd stuck with the fore-and-aft design there just wouldn't have been enough challenge for them after the first few days.

The next stage was to find a builder. Now, this was well before the days of New Zealand's burgeoning superyacht industry, and 'Lou's dream' was the largest sailing vessel to be built in this country for about thirty years. It wasn't a job for just any boat builder. So we contacted Len Brijs who had just shifted his yard into Vos's yard to form the company Vos and Brijs. Len and I had worked together for two years so we knew each other well.

Building the ship was very much a team effort. The staff at the yard put their heart and soul into the project. Several people deserve special mention. Draughtsman John Walker was invaluable when it came to designing new fittings. Engineer Tony Irvine did a great job of the installation. John Street of Fosters Ship Chandlers gave me free rein of his chandlery. I had a fabulous time scavenging in his cellars for old pieces of equipment left over from the scow days, which John very reasonably let me buy at cost price. Many other wonderful people let me twist their arms to supply us with the items we needed.

Many things that we did on the 'fine lady' are now benchmark practices in today's shipbuilding. The holding

Trainees on the first girls' voyage, Coromandel, June 1974.

tanks are a good example. At the time, *Spirit of Adventure* was only the second vessel built in New Zealand to install holding tanks.

You don't start building a ship of this size without the media sniffing around. They would come to the yard and ask what we were building (as if it wasn't apparent) and for whom. I would tell them that we were building a yacht for 'Sir' Louis Fisher's family and they would print this. That caused some embarrassment! But in my opinion, if any businessman deserved a knighthood it was Lou, for taking the gamble to provide such a fine vessel for the youth of New Zealand.

We launched the ship eighteen months after construction started. Normally an undertaking of that kind would take about two and a half years, but not with Lou driving it! It was just go, go, go over that period, with barely enough time in the day to draw breath. I was still finishing off in the engine room two months after the ship was launched, and we couldn't hoist all the sails for the first few voyages as the rigging wasn't finished.

How did I become master/engineer for those first voyages? Lou's original intention was to employ a naval officer as captain and to use me in the role of sailing master. But at that time most naval officers didn't have the certificates that the Marine Department required. I had the right tickets so I was in the hot seat. After a couple of voyages, Lou and the Trust Board agreed, reluctantly, to install me as permanent master/engineer for the Gulf area that the ship was surveyed for.

Very conscious of our public image, we put everything into those early voyages. There was huge media interest. They circled us like hawks, waiting for us on the wharf when we returned from a voyage. Unfortunately, as today, much of their interest seemed to be in bad news stories. 'Have you drowned anyone yet?' seemed to be their unspoken question at the end of each voyage.

We pushed everyone very hard in those early years — design, building, commissioning, those first voyages. In some ways I don't know how we got away with it, but we did. The challenges seemed insurmountable some days. It might look reasonably easy now when the Trust is a well-established, highly respected organisation, but back at the start we were literally learning by doing. Remember, all the old-timers who knew anything about square rig were long dead! There hadn't been a square-rigger in New Zealand waters for over fifty years.

Lou's original concept — how strange it seems now — was to build a ship to give New Zealand's *young men* the chance to go to sea in a sailing ship. After a few voyages we started to get young ladies coming to the wharf to ask when they were going to have a turn. I put this proposal to the Trust Board and they originally cried it down. Only men sailed ships!

But the girls soon got their turn, on voyage 11. Unfortunately it was a mid-winter voyage and a gale blew up. The two anchors failed to hold the ship and off she went out to sea. Our radio at the time was good for only a couple of miles and we lost contact with the shore. The office staff of one (how times have changed!), James Lennox-King, had so many phone calls about our safety that when we got back next day the news media descended on us, hoping to get a sensational story. What they found was a bunch of excited young women saying what a great time they'd had. With lots of photos in the Sunday papers, the girls made sure they were going to get the chance to sail the ship regularly. I had to come to grips with taking women to sea as well.

After 21 voyages on the trot (there were no employment contracts in those days), I decided it was time to move on to a job that gave my family more financial stability and more chance of seeing me at home. I continued to fill in as relieving master for a while after I left.

How has the organisation changed over time? I think the major change has been in philosophy. It very soon became obvious that the 'Spirit experience' was about much more than just giving kids the chance to learn to sail. And so the Trust developed into a youth development organisation. We added activities: tramping, rowing, team-building exercises. In the early days many of the people involved with *Spirit* had army backgrounds and they were a great source of ideas for activities.

Originally the trainees spent a large part of each voyage in the aft cabin sitting through formal lectures. We soon realised that learning by doing was a far better way of getting the message across and teaching things that just couldn't be taught in the classroom.

Trainee Day is a good example of how we learned along the way. Nick Hylton is responsible for instigating Trainee Day in a formal sense, but we had our own Trainee Day right back at the beginning. On Voyage 2 a rather slow kid came up to me and said, 'I can be captain.' I called his bluff and said, 'Right, be captain then. Find yourself a cook and an engineer and get on with it.' Ron Bird, who had taken over as engineer by then, liked what he saw and set up a sort of Trainee Day from Voyage 4. It just built up from there and became a nucleus for learning, a goal for the end of the trip.

Mate Chris Oliver instructing trainees in navigation, early voyage of *Spirit of Adventure*.

THE SPIRIT OF SQUARE RIG

JOHN DUDER

John Duder, civil engineer and Hauraki Gulf yachtsman, joined the Trust Board in 1975, and today, apart from chairman Stephen Fisher, remains as the longest-serving trustee. He was for many years chairman of the training committee, and has also undertaken numerous voyages on both ships as a volunteer mate.

WHY THIS FASCINATION with square rig? It was a defining moment when *Spirit of Adventure*'s designer Jack Brooke added one single yard to the initial ketch rig sail plan. She became a schooner, then Jack cut the plan in half and added ten feet (literally — the plan exists). Another yard, added with considerable encouragement from Barry Thompson, made her a topsail schooner or possibly, if we are being pedantic here, a brigantine.

In the 1970s square rig was seen as an anachronism, at least in the 'British' world, which had since the 1890s turned its back on training its naval officers under sail. The Scandinavians, South Americans and others continued to recognise the unique value of square rig in sail training. So we began on *Spirit of Adventure*; older hands will recall the hoisting of the three square sails, course, topsail and raffee, from the deck, believe it or not, like so much laundry. What potential for twists, fouled headsail rigging and so on — not to mention that original head stick on the raffee.

Meanwhile the Sail Training Association in Britain, from which some of the Spirit Trust's motivation had come, had got really brave and bent *Sir Winston Churchill*'s topsail to its yard. This required a whole different set of confusing lines, mysteriously known as braces, bunt lines, clew lines, etc, and actually required people to go aloft, a dangerously archaic activity.

This 'breakthrough' of course merely repeated the historic evolution and refinement of square rig from the earliest Mediterranean ships through the progressive introduction of foot ropes in the fifteenth century to reduce the risk inherent in balancing on the yard while furling (although in fairness, medieval squares were clewed to the bunt — for evidence, refer to any number of galleon paintings by Dutch masters and their peers). Back ropes were introduced on training ships last century and finally personal harnesses after World War Two, their worth underscored by tragic deaths or injury even in quite recent times on some stubborn ships not too far from our shores.

The fact is that a set of squares properly and safely rigged, calling on centuries of hard-won experience, is more controllable than the equivalent large gaff mainsail and topsail (witness *Spirit of New Zealand* once breaking her main gaff in a gybe), and is more readily reduced in area. Except when really close hauled, square rig is as, if not more, efficient.

But this does not explain the fascination with square rig. Do we retain atavistic memories of fishermen standing up on a bundle of reeds or a coracle with a woven mat or animal skin, or of our ancestors' voyages to foreign shores? Part of it is the sheer beauty and exhilaration of a barque or ship-rigged vessel under full sail — felt by many to be one of mankind's finest creations, working with nature rather than against it, and demanding immense skill and physical stamina.

Come the 1980s, with topsail and course firmly bent on *Spirit of Adventure*, the Spirit Trust had the confidence to rig *Spirit of New Zealand* as a barquentine, confirming square rig as a key element of our enterprise. For trainees, going aloft is part of their ten-day voyage experience, but control of enthusiastic climbers has become a safety issue on weekend and public sailings. Of many memories of gulf and coastal voyages in both our ships, one in particular is of a trainee on *Spirit of Adventure* from Lyttelton to Port Chalmers. Our first night saw a brisk sail to the east side of Lyttelton Harbour in a 40-knot southerly with hail, and a first climb aloft in the dark with some of my watch to furl the topsail. A boy who had not had the easiest of voyages told me when signing off in Dunedin that being aloft on the yard that night was his best memory of the voyage.

How handy *Spirit of Adventure*'s single topsail could be! Roaring into what seemed a crowded anchorage in Whangamumu Harbour, we backed the topsail in a fresh northerly to bring her smartly to a halt as heads popped out of yacht companionways. It features in my shots from the bowsprit and the lee deck as Raoul Island appeared through an evening rain squall on the ship's penultimate voyage under our flag, and when we hove to for 'crossing the date line'. That ceremony brings back memories of a very special cadet, Nigel Cooper, killed in a tragic Cook Strait ferry accident, not long after leaving the Spirit of Adventure Trust to pursue a seafaring career.

Square rig properly if briefly returned to New Zealand with the Whangarei building of the second *Bounty* film replica and her commissioning in 1978. Spotting her profile while on a job at Marsden Power Station, set against Bream Head and the offshore islands exactly as Cook's *Endeavour* would have appeared 200 years before, I begged myself aboard for the next two days of sea trials, and just happened to be on the wheel when she did the first full tack under full sail. 'Helm's down!' All squares a-back, quickly reverse the helm for a stern board ... lee fore brace and headsail sheets (to get the foremast sails drawing on a new tack) ... mainsail haul ... and we were off into a north-east rain squall. The rig had been set up by that master rigger with whom I'd sailed on *Norsaga*, Harry Spencer, from Cowes on the Isle of Wight; but the inevitable stretch of the brand new rigging had the fore topmast bending to the extent that the huge deep single topsail and its yard had to be struck in a hurry — so much so that the TV crews missed the action and the language,

The first occasion on which *Spirit of Adventure* sailed with 'all sails set', including the lower square sails (course and topsail) and the raffee with head stick. Man O'War Bay to Motuihe Island, Voyage 13, August 1974. (Ron Bird)

and asked if the boys could do it again for the cameras. The response was akin to that when Team New Zealand lost their mast.

The next day was a real photo opportunity for shots from the topgallant mast and end of jibboom, and Cliff Hawkins set off in the ship's boat to add to his collection of timeless images.

On both tacks *Bounty* had been braced up hard, with the yards on the backstays, yet we only ended up where we had started under Bream Head, so how did such a vessel make to windward at all? The answer did not come until her voyage across the Pacific under Paul Leppington; the jeers — tackles that hold the course (lower) yards against the masts — broke and allowed the yards to hang clear of the masts. This allowed those deep topsails to be braced around harder and she began to make to windward.

The film ship *Bounty* was crewed mainly by *Spirit of Adventure* boys — no girls in the late '70s — who entered into the spirit of eighteenth century sailing with the appropriate archaic language, complete with cat o' nine tails and lashings of tomato sauce for the photographer. One small passenger did not survive the last day of sail trials; a possum had nestled in the furled main course, despite strict overnight security, and after being harassed by TV cameramen trying to interview it, descended the rigging, sat briefly on a revolving capstan, and finally took refuge under the jibboom, from where it was presumably shaken into the sea by the flogging of headsails during that first tack.

Spirit of New Zealand was commissioned on a cold squally day in August 1986 after a staunch gang of volunteers, all women under

Spirit of Adventure's foremast from the mainmast upper crosstree. (John Duder)

the direction of mate Margaret Pidgeon, had worked overnight to place and epoxy-cement an extra 15 tons of iron pigs into the keel. Then, with her bright new set of sails including topsail and topgallant, Captain Nick Hylton took us out for the first memorable sail. The sound of flogging spinnakers and broaching yachts to windward heralded a strong squall ('stand to your clews and bunts'), but Nick let her run on ('best to find out if anything is wrong now') and shortly afterward came his excited call from the wheelhouse: 'Fifteen knots!' The speedo probably had not been fine-tuned, but it sure felt like fifteen knots.

Here finally was a real square-rigger, and thanks to some prodding by Paul Leppington, I got my restricted launch master's ticket to sail as a mate in the Gulf and on the East Coast. So it was that a dream became a reality. My first voyage on a square-rigger as a first mate was a day trip out of Whitianga, a particularly appropriate circumstance, as Buffalo Beach just happens to be where great-grandfather Thomas Duder was shipwrecked on the full-rigged ship HMS *Buffalo* in 1840. His youngest son, my grandfather, travelled several times around the Horn in square rig, and my father twice worked his passage to England in cargo ships.

Perhaps the Trust really came of age when *Spirit of New Zealand* sailed to Australia in 1988 as New Zealand's flagship for the bicentenary celebrations. In Melbourne she was voted the most appropriate training ship by the fairly demanding Dutch, on the look-out for a new ship; out of Hobart she won the start with an extraordinary tack by sailing master Nick Hylton, in what I swear was no wind at all, and was second in her class into Sydney behind Australia's new brigantine *Young Endeavour* — certainly a fast ship but with none of *Spirit's* style, and trainees considerably older than ours.

Who will forget those timeless shots of the new millennium dawn off Gisborne, *Spirit of New Zealand* and *Søren Larsen* flanked by sailing waka?

For those lucky enough to sail on her, the Australian

SAIL TRAINING

Trainees arrive, often after travelling overnight, to gaze upwards in amazement at the rig of each vessel. They wonder at the complexity of it all and very soon are involved in the machine we call the 'Spirit experience'.

Wonder turns into inquisitiveness as stores, equipment and the joining routine take over. New names to learn; awkward, unfamiliar language to decipher.

The mystery unfolds as we explain about leaving egos, boyfriends, chewing gum and society on the wharf and gaining the benefits of 'our' ship society, a new fresh way of looking at life, no swearing, no pressure from peer groups or exams, no hassles from ardent pursuants. Here they may be free to enjoy the experience and establish once again their own identity, be their own self without the 'mark' they found themselves using. All that matters is that the ship demands the group or family succeeding together.

Ten days later the family returns, ostensibly the same group — but subtly and fundamentally changed, more laughter, more smiles, more real expression and free exchange of warm embraces. Sure, they know a lot about sailing and outdoors, but most of all they have learned about themselves by a combination of sandpaper and love. Sail training.

PAUL LEPPINGTON

replica of James Cook's HMB *Endeavour* would have to be the ultimate square-rig experience. I will long remember the 12 to 4 night watch after leaving Whitianga for Tauranga, our watch familiar enough with that maze of lines after only three days, with no lights other than for navigation, wearing ship to a light northerly. The quiet orders, not changed in 200 years, to a timeless orchestration of wood and canvas — the nearest to a time warp one could experience.

LEARNING THROUGH EXPERIENCE

JIM LOTT

Jim Lott is widely known in maritime circles as a Spirit of Adventure Trust volunteer, one of the very earliest, also as a teacher of navigation and seamanship and builder/skipper of a strong and handsome yacht, Victoria, *in which he and his family did a two-year world cruise. He now works for the Maritime Safety Authority. Beginning as a mate, he became a relieving master for the Trust in 1997 on both ten-day voyages and day sails.*

DURING 1971, Auckland sailors became aware of an unusually large new sailing ship being built by Lou Fisher in St Mary's Bay.

I wandered along and looked up at a steel wall so much larger than anything previously encountered. At the time my wife Karin and I had just bought the 31-foot Woollacott cutter *Vectis* and were in the process of a major rebuild. I had sailed from the Pacific Islands to New Zealand some years previously and *Vectis* was intended to take us on a long family cruise.

The Chilean ship *Esmeralda* had visited New Zealand, countless sailing ship and yachting books had been digested and now we were to have our own sailing ship. It was a stirring time for a young fellow impatient to spend time under sail at sea. But little did I ever expect to become involved.

An old family friend, James Lennox-King, phoned late in 1973 and asked if I could give a hand on the auspicious day the new *Spirit of Adventure* was to be launched. How lucky can a young fellow be? Along with a bunch of other young Auckland sailors, we climbed the long ladder to lay out mooring lines and other important tasks. It was explained that only one or two could stay aboard, since launching such a vessel was outside the experience of all concerned and no one really knew what would happen.

Speeches always seem long to young people, then *Spirit* reluctantly inched along the rail tracks. The view from the front row of well-wishers of her spectacular plunge to the sea was imprinted on my memory, with a wave sweeping the deck from stern to bow. Her subsequent charge among the spectator fleet provided plenty of excitement and lots to talk about, once we had secured the mooring lines.

James, now ensconced at the Marsden Wharf office as operations director, rang again a few months later and in April 1974 I was back aboard for a voyage as third mate. That was the lowest position in those days. I think it may have been Voyage 7. Leaving Karin at home alone with a son a few months old did not provide her with unmitigated joy.

My first task on sailing day was to go aloft and mouse a series of shackles on the newly crossed yards. I also had to secure the vertical pins in the cranes holding the yards on the aluminium foremast. The ship's tool kit comprised little more than pliers, spanner and screwdriver and not a sign of seizing wire. A wire coat-hanger did sterling duty for the cranes, and I was sent to a local ship chandler's to buy some seizing wire. There was no money in the petty cash tin but I had more than sufficient for the small purchase. James apologised for the imposition and presented me with a tie. I still wear the tie, so I came out well ahead on the transaction.

The master was John Littler who, after retirement from the navy, had sailed his yacht from Canada to New Zealand. The mate, who also had the task of engineer, was Glen Cornthwaite, later sadly to be lost at sea on a yacht delivery voyage. I recall we also had a second mate and a cook who left after a few days, with the second mate then adding cooking duties to his schedule. Of course, no girls or women were considered suitable for a voyage in those days. It was not until Naomi James became the first woman to sail solo around the world in 1978 that the myth of male supremacy at sea was finally put to rest. In

The official party just before the launch of *Spirit of Adventure*, 8 December 1973.

April 1974 the notion of a female master on *Spirit* was about as ridiculous as imagining New Zealand could win the America's Cup.

So, with the boys divided into three watches each led by a mate, we headed out from Marsden Wharf. About ten minutes later the ship received a tersely worded telegram from Mr Fisher reminding us that all crew and trainees were to be dressed in 'whites' when departing or arriving.

There was no programme as such, but the emphasis was on the lads learning as much as possible about sailing, staying fit and having fun. We sent them on walks on the Gulf islands, swimming, sailing in small fiberglass dories, tying knots and anything else we could dream up. All the time we ran an inter-watch competition with a cup to be awarded at the end of the voyage. This certainly maintained the trainees' enthusiasm; now, there's no inter-watch competition though there are individual awards.

Towards the end of the voyage we were coming in the passage north of Kawau Island, bowling along in a fair breeze. Although the yards were crossed (i.e. hoisted into place), we had no square sails aboard. The master told us he knew the area well and had lined us up to pass between Kawati Point and the rock about a half-cable north, a passage with no room for error. As we ground to a sudden halt, the rock just under the surface was clear to all. With sails lying where they were dropped and the bowsprit angled high, we tried in vain to use stern power. A passing trawler took the end of a mooring line to give a hand. The flooding tide carried the hawser round our turning propeller; as our engine stopped, silence descended.

The *Spirit*s have always brought out the best in people; a diver from one of the many spectator craft which had appeared from nowhere soon had the rope free and stayed handy to make a check on the hull once we were afloat. He reported, 'Just a scratch down the keel.'

At Mansion House I was delegated to report the mishap to 'head office' by phone. James Lennox-King responded, 'If there's no hole in the bottom, I'm far more interested in finding a crew for the next trip than knowing you sat on a rock.' So ended what was perhaps the ship's first major grounding.

When I rejoined *Spirit* about three years later following a cruise in the Pacific, quite a few changes were apparent. We had a steel foremast, no staysail boom and no dories. James had retired and we were making the most of the ship by running weekend voyages for the increasing numbers of people attending navigation classes run in Auckland night schools. Using volunteers to run the ship for these supplementary voyages was a decision that was to have far-reaching benefits.

One thing that has never changed is our need to learn as we go along. At that time, experience in sail-training ships was available to very few of us, so the ability to learn from each other as we made many mistakes contributed to the strength the Spirit organisation has today. Other sailing organisations which have not had a foundation of volunteers have denied themselves the depth and breadth of knowledge provided by the talents of our many willing helpers who have elected to be involved.

The resurgence of traditional sailing vessels, especially square-rigged ships, is a splendid trend while the world around seems so focused on small screens to provide us with knowledge and understanding. However, technology is unable to provide any knowledge or understanding of ourselves as people. A sailing vessel at sea still has few equals in providing such insight.

One of the most frequent volunteer masters was Con Thode, who in his unassuming way has been such a mentor to all who have had the privilege of sailing with him on the wide variety of vessels he has commanded. Con has the knack of running a 'happy ship', which to my mind equates to efficiency and good seamanship. His yarns of yachting, workboats and, of course, his war experiences in submarines are an entertainment and an education covering almost a century.

One long weekend when Con was master, we were safely anchored in a sheltered spot at Great Barrier Island. Outside, it was blowing a solid gale from the east. We had to head back and it made sense to cross Colville Channel and head south in the sheltered water off Coromandel. Well reefed down, we soon reached flat water, and lighter winds prompted us to set some squares and the jib. With half the crew at lunch, we sailed quietly along with the occasional puff over Moehau causing us to heel a little from time to time. One of those at lunch asked how far the ship could heel safely. 'Don't worry till the water covers the saloon windows' was the tongue-in-cheek reply.

About a minute or so later the water was indeed lapping at the sills. Those on deck managed to let go a sheet or two and the ship soon righted herself. Aboard were members of the Bucklands Beach Yacht Club who reacted sensibly and kept an eye out for people overboard and so on. Some had clambered outside the rails. We later measured that the water had been up to the window sills round the cabin to a depth of seven feet at the gunwale, and that we had heeled through 55° with the course yard arm, well braced, actually awash. *Spirit of Adventure* was soundly designed and built and could recover from a much greater angle of heel, but it felt pretty scary at the time.

At this time we had a strong-willed (some would say ferocious) operations director, Bob Lawry. With his almost parsimonious management, the Trust's bank balance was healthy, but we were all subject to a stern telling off for what seemed trifling incidents. Once the ship was secured after the knock-down, discussion centred on how we were going to avoid a thorough dressing down from Bob. The mate's starboard cabin had suffered a similar fate to the engine room and everything was soaked. But Bob's

sharp eye spotted a soggy mattress being carried into the shed and the cat was out of the bag.

Again we learned a great deal from the experience. We now appreciated why sailing ships generally have the sheets of square sails belayed to the mast pin-rails so they are not submerged during a knock-down. One of the most important points we had not really focused on till then was the engine ventilation system. The water was up to the floor plates in the engine room and had down-flooded through the air intakes located along the sides of the deckhouse. Even a small amount of flooding can dramatically decrease a ship's stability. The important thing is that the organisation not only learned from experience, but acted as a result. Much insight from operating *Spirit of Adventure* was incorporated into the building of *Spirit of New Zealand*. In time, the next ship will be a further improvement, but only if we retain and use the wealth of knowledge both paid and volunteer crews have gained, and continue to gain, when a design brief is prepared.

It is our good fortune to have had two immensely talented senior masters. While Nick Hylton has never claimed to be an academic, he commands everyone's respect as a natural intuitive seaman. When he joined in 1979, he was exactly right for the time, raising the standards of the crew and ensuring both volunteers and paid crew worked together harmoniously for the good of the trainees and the organisation. His successor, Paul Leppington, is also a superb instinctive seaman and has used his talents to lead the on-board operation of the ships through a period of great change, with society being so much more demanding of individuals and organisations. One wonders if there exists anywhere a person with as much knowledge and expertise in rigging sailing ships. Having two outstanding sailors in such a crucial role has ensured essential continuity.

The great changes in our organisation have had to take place to keep abreast of the enormous changes in New Zealand society and culture since the 1970s and avoid fading into obscurity, or worse, failing to sustain the strictest standards of safety and maintenance. One suspects there will have to be even greater changes in the future. Thinking back 25 years, computers and electronic

Captains Paul Leppington and Nick Hylton confer on the day of *Spirit of New Zealand*'s first sea trials.

navigation as we know it were yet to arrive, shops were closed at weekends and there were few adventure-type activities available to youth or adults. It was relatively easy to fill the ship with enthusiastic trainees; we did not have to compete with the plethora of adrenalin-producing activities now on offer. Nor did we have to compete with the entertainment provided indoors by the ubiquitous small screen and its stunning ability to occupy the mind.

Society makes increasing demands that all physical activity is rendered totally safe, with severe penalties for mistakes or oversight. Many of the things we used to do to stimulate young minds and bodies are now forbidden, and we hear some male youths advising that what we offer on a youth development voyage is 'boring'. It's to the

credit of the crew that they have developed so many tough challenges, with danger perceived but not real. It's noticeable that females, once thought unsuitable for voyages, now often prove more enthusiastic and capable than their male counterparts. Again this seems to mirror society as a whole.

With the launch of *Spirit of New Zealand* in 1986 we found a whole new set of challenges requiring a very steep learning curve. There were plenty of teething problems, some major, many minor, and some which provided a stern test. Barry Thompson, who has given a great deal of his life to the Trust and its ships, provided leadership and wisdom to us all.

Barry's first voyage after recovering from a heart attack

was also his first voyage in *Spirit of New Zealand*. It was summer and we decided we would take things quietly and work well 'inside the envelope'. We were quietly sailing across the Gulf when both of us noticed a group of adult trainees enjoying cans of beer on the bowsprit. Such is not what is expected or allowed, and Barry sets and expects very high standards. However, the transgressors were quickly advised and totally cooperative.

The next test came that evening when the main engine suddenly stopped half-way up Bon Accord Harbour at Kawau Island. Coming off the wind, we set some sail and headed for Mahurangi with the expectation of having our engine soon operating. This was not to be, and as we tacked up Mahurangi Harbour to a suitable anchoring spot, all electrics failed including the depth finder.

Safely anchored, we set about finding the problem with the sea-water section of the engine cooling system. It turned out to be an airlock, but we were unable to diagnose this at the time. We knew that we could sail back to Auckland and still have sufficient use of the engine to berth safely.

I was forward as we very gently came alongside. We were getting lines ashore nicely with just a few metres to go when I noticed us pick up speed. With a bump seeming inevitable, we asked those on the foredeck to move quickly aft as our bowsprit penetrated deeply into a window of the Watersiders' Union building ahead. Fortunately, no one was aloft.

Eventually we stopped. We secured alongside with many observers wide-eyed and silent. Barry commented that he was quite bewildered as to what caused the accident, until the engineer admitted he had gone ahead on the engine control when it should have been in neutral. This mistake was certainly understandable given the then unusual mounting of the engine control lever, and the fact that the ship had only just been brought into commission. So a quiet weekend became one of the most action-filled on record, and Barry's heart certainly withstood quite a few heart-stopping moments.

We all have moments when we would like to swallow some words just uttered, and no one is exempt from 'foot-in-mouth' disease. During a day sail on Whangarei Harbour some of the more adventurous passengers were aloft taking off gaskets. One man was on the royal yard when a woman came up to me by the wheel and made a comment about how high he was. Facetiously I said he was probably singing 'Nearer my God to Thee'. She looked somewhat quizzical and said, 'That's my husband, and he's a vicar.'

In recent years the organisation has strongly encouraged all its sea-going masters and mates to try to gain as much knowledge as possible. The first Square Rig Endorsement classes held in Auckland in 1996 were very successful, with most achieving a pass mark in both exams. The course was anything but easy. A huge amount of detail had to be absorbed and understood. It's easy to become a bit complacent and the course quickly deflated any egos. Rarely have so many nervous masters been gathered together in one place. Much coffee and many late night study sessions were needed. But the knowledge of all was raised another notch, and with it both the safety of the ship and the enthusiasm for giving the trainees a more memorable experience.

The one thing that all the volunteers who have served alongside the permanent crew have in common is enthusiasm. Certainly there is a wide variety of talent in the seamanship sense, but no matter how capable anyone is, without enthusiasm for the trainees and the experience we can provide, they may as well stay home.

All who crew in *Spirit* on a regular basis are rewarded in some way. To see a group of youngsters nervously board, looking about for someone who might be a friend, then contrast this scene with the last day, gives us all a great deal of confidence in the future. It is particularly rewarding to see those from less privileged backgrounds gaining pride and self-esteem as they realise how well they can cope, provided they try. Seeing those used to an affluent lifestyle drop away the trappings and appreciate that, for the voyage, all that counts is what they do aboard, aptly demonstrates the concept of youth development at its best. When the trainees from these different extremes of background leave the ship with a mutual respect and a brief vision of how life can be, we know it is an experience they will remember and be better for.

KIDS *CAN* DO IT!

NICK HYLTON

Nick Hylton trained as a paramedic with the US Army, sailed in the great American maxi yachts Kialoa *and* Ondine, *completed three circumnavigations and worked on charter boats in the Caribbean, Indian Ocean and Fiji before he came to live in New Zealand in 1977. During his twelve years with the Trust, he sailed nearly 200 voyages as master and senior master on both* Spirit of Adventure *and* Spirit of New Zealand. *Later he gained a first mate foreign-going certificate and worked in trans-Tasman container ships.*

A MOMENT OF TRUTH came during one of my first two voyages on *Spirit of Adventure* in 1979, those that I did as a mate while getting the necessary ticket to sail as master on Voyage 126.

I can remember Jim Revell, ex-Navy, standing in front of these trainees and giving a detailed description of a windlass — the gypsy and the spider, all the workings. And I'm watching these youngsters sitting there scribbling this down, and I'm thinking, why am I here? What is this for? What's the relevance? Well, then we got them all out, got them all seasick, put them through the routine and sailed around the Gulf. But I'm thinking there's more to life than that, surely more things these trainees can do.

Long-time master Nick Hylton on board *Spirit of New Zealand*. **'I am altering course to starboard!'**

programme that was under constant review and improvement by myself and the group of talented mates we had at the time, assessing what worked and what didn't.

Until then, the final day was a games day — we'd put the kids ashore on a nice beach, sail around in small boats, play ball games, tug of war, that sort of thing. But I figured, they can do that any place, and if it's really miserable weather, what then? So why don't we just go sailing, and then, why don't you guys elect somebody to be skipper, and from there it evolved into what we have today.

Key people during this evolutionary period were Gordon Ingram and Heidi Richardson, Naomi Petersen, Janet Watkins, Graham Lyons, Bruce McGhee, Jennifer Roberts, Liz England, later Margaret Pidgeon. Those last three all had teaching backgrounds, which was obviously helpful. We drew on all our strengths. I remember first asking the engineer Jim Pretty to give a talk. He quickly declined, but then we got him talking about steam in the old days, how big those machines were, and the trainees were absolutely rapt.

Trainee Day, as far as I know, is unique to the two *Spirit* ships, but it didn't just happen. There was no voyage when we first said to the trainees on day one, 'On day nine you guys are going to sail this ship yourselves, with your own elected officers, using the skills and knowledge you've acquired by then.' Trainee Day evolved gradually over probably two or three years, as part of the training

Concentration is etched on the face of a trainee climbing the rigging of *Spirit of New Zealand*. (Andy Belcher)

From the start, I had made some interesting discoveries. One of the most significant occurred when we were on a trip out at Waiheke. The trainees had finished lunch, and the wind had sprung up and we said, 'Oh, we've got some wind out there, let's go for a sail!' The trainees said they'd just had lunch, and they didn't want to go sailing. Trying to be helpful, I said 'Look, we'll show you how fast we can do it.' So Gordon, Heidi, the cook and I got out there and had everything up in about four minutes, mainsail, up

with the whole works, even the topsail set. We went sailing off — and the look on the trainees' faces said it all. 'They don't need us.' And I swore never to do that again. If you show them how easy it is for a skilled individual, they'll never try, and they'll never make it. Learning is always step by step.

We learned that the election of the trainee skipper and officers needed careful management, though of course we were not present at the actual election. Initially their choice was always the most popular person, not who would sail the best, or the most competent. So we began to say to them, you need someone who is capable of handling the vessel, not necessarily the most popular. And remember your first mate is also very important. So, having given them a more descriptive idea of the people they needed to handle these jobs properly, all of a sudden we started to get female skippers.

The choice of trainee skipper was either surprising or predictable, about 50/50. Quite often it was someone who'd been quiet; their watch officer probably knew who they were, but I, looking over the entire group, might not have picked them out. All of a sudden this individual would come out and I would check with the watch officer, who would say 'Yeah, he or she has been right behind the whole group, keeping it together.'

I was continually amazed by the respect they had for the job — the anguish, the level of responsibility. This was true not only of the master but also the mate, and the elected cooks, navigators and engineers. They'd say, 'I didn't realise how much was involved. Is that what I have to do?' And they'd come back at the end and say 'Thank you, I understand a lot more than I did before.'

This rubbed off on other trainees. After the election, I'd get the group of officers together and say, 'Listen, it is vital that you work as a team. If you leave all of the responsibility to your elected captain, if you don't feed them any information, it's going to fall apart. So the responsibility for all of the trainees in your watch is with you, not just the captain. You'd better make sure you understand that.'

Some of the navigators had unbelievably bad times. I'd hear cries of 'You sure we're here?' 'No, we can't be, look at that island', and so on. And through them I could feed a lot of information to the skipper, sharing the level of responsibility. I used to say, 'It may appear to you that I'm dictating what happens on this ship, but I'm not. In fact the crew sits around the table at mealtimes doing exactly what you guys are doing — conferring to find out who's doing what and where, and who's the best to handle this.'

Safety was of course always the primary factor. The adult crew never completely disappeared. If I wasn't on deck, I was in the wheelhouse keeping an eye on things. You could describe it as loose cover only, especially in areas or weather conditions where very little danger actually existed. We've had fewer accidents than some other square-rigged sail-training ships, because we did everything with all safety aspects correctly covered.

If we had to intervene, we did. On *Spirit of New Zealand*, I think somewhere around Waiheke about 1986, the ship was approaching an anchorage at a speed that meant that they had to drop the topsail and the topgallant, and get them both to back so we'd slow down enough. Otherwise we were going to touch bottom.

I just quietly said to the elected skipper, 'You know, we're moving quite fast and it's very shallow out here. If you watch that little gauge over there it'll tell you the depth of the water — and when it reads zero, we're going to be stuck.' At this there were panic noises — but I knew the tide was coming in and said, 'What are you going to do now?' They got quite excited and upset. I said, '*Don't* drop the anchor' — they were all ready to go — and we backed out and everything was fine. That was a programmed accident, which shouldn't have happened, but it did.

On other occasions, when I could see that they were not aware that vessels make leeway and they were trying to tack out of a passage, I used to ask, 'Do you think you'll have enough room over there?' By asking the quiet question, you make them alert to the possibilities.

Sure, it was hard at the beginning for adults to stand back and listen, reminding themselves, *don't* tell the trainees what to do, let them make their mistakes. But then we started to get some of the more enlightened crew who understood the new approach and knew that most of the time you didn't have to say too much, other than when you could see a problem developing you could quietly say, 'If you take that sheet or hitch off too soon, you'll get hurt.'

We also emphasised that this was not a school ship, and we're not going to *tell* you what to do. But, if you want to go from A to B, you have to accept certain responsibilities for learning.

With *Spirit of New Zealand* in 1986, we moved to mixed voyages. At the first swim the make-up disappears,

My reason for writing is to say how impressed I am with the whole Spirit of Adventure *programme.*

I heard many of the [Sail Training Association] team — and there were several of us in Australia — express their admiration for your new ship; for the many new ideas incorporated in the ship; for the behaviour and enthusiasm of the young crew; for the close links that you have established with your government departments and for the willingness of your Board members and staff to share their experience and knowledge with others working in the same field.

I do congratulate you and your Board for the great amount that you are achieving.

FROM JOHN H HAMILTON, RACE DIRECTOR, THE SAIL TRAINING ASSOCIATION (UNITED KINGDOM) TO THE TRUST BOARD, FOLLOWING SPIRIT OF NEW ZEALAND'S PARTICIPATION IN THE AUSTRALIAN BICENTENARY.

along with all decorative plumage that has arrived on board. For a couple of days they've been seasick and they're hanging over the side, so by about the fifth day everyone has settled down into team activity where it doesn't matter who you are, male or female. You'd pull on this, clean that, and it was all incorporated with the learning.

On the unisex voyages on *Spirit of Adventure* some differences between the boys' and girls' trips were mind-blowing. The girls came on thinking that they would have a new experience, but certainly they couldn't handle the ship, no way. That was just one of those things girls couldn't do. When they achieved that goal, the sense of accomplishment was ten thousand times more than the boys. The boys would say, 'Well, yeah, we did it.'

I've been asked why, if our training programme and Trainee Day concept is so well tested and so successful, other youth development ships have not followed suit.

It's partly the age group, which is significantly younger than similar ships in Australia, and brings on board kids used to working in group situations. Partly also that we draw a wide range of kids with greatly differing back-

grounds from a whole country, urban and rural. I don't think it would work with the same age group drawn from Auckland only. We did have some trips at exam time where most trainees were Aucklanders, and they never worked as well. If we dealt only with city kids it would be a different training programme — probably something markedly different. The rural youngsters do chores in the morning, so when the city kids suddenly see these rural kids sleeping next to them, rising at six and getting going without any hesitation, they go along with it. This peer pressure takes the burden off the crew from spending unnecessary time and effort on getting the best out of the city youngsters. They say to themselves, 'Yep, there are merits in this, I can do this, I can do the swim and I won't die, so let's get on with it.'

I only had one Trainee Day that didn't happen. I was once flabbergasted by a group that just did not want to go sailing. They wanted a beach party, so we had a beach party. It was their day. We said, 'Fine' — but we were thinking '*What?*!' — and put them on the beach. I had to stick to my guns. Did they regret this later? I don't think so. It was a city group.

Individual 'failures' were very rare. One lad on a southern voyage from Dunedin to Bluff and Stewart Island got up to day six without participating in anything. It wasn't his thing. About all Hamish did was eat — and the food didn't taste all that good to him. He didn't want to clean up, didn't want to do anything. So I got together with all the trainees (but not Hamish) in the aft cabin and said 'Listen, you guys have got to make a decision. Is Hamish going to stay? Remember, he needs a partner and whoever his partner is is going to be suffering because he's holding things up, and it's getting into conflict, people are starting to get physical. We can put him ashore. If he wants to go that's fine, and if he doesn't we'll send him ashore anyway.' They all cried with one voice, 'Yes, get him off!'

So we sent him ashore. That was a real eye-opener for me, having never had to land a youngster before, and it only happened to me one other time. Hamish was totally unapproachable — although avid about what he wanted in life and how he wanted to do it, nothing on board the ship matched. His parents wanted him to come out on the voyage because he'd been home taught and hadn't had much to do with other people, so it was written on the wall. He just couldn't assimilate that fast, although given more time, he may have. I thought I had him one morning when he went for a swim ... but landing him was totally a trainee decision, conscientiously arrived at after five or six days of working through it.

Any perception that the *Spirit* ships have developed a programme which could be described as 'fun in the sun' is simply uninformed of what actually happens on board. I think the 'fun' notion may be something to do with the length of time *Spirit* spends in the relatively benign northern waters of the Hauraki Gulf rather than doing long coastal trips, not being out at sea every night, laying hove to in storms.

Teenagers have a different mode for recounting their experiences. This age group says, 'Yes, I had a great time, I made such great friends.' They tend not to say, 'I

Trainees paddling the 'rubber duckie', Leigh Marine Reserve, 1997.

learned how to navigate and furl a sail.' For us, furling a sail is not the most important thing. Our emphasis is on personal growth rather than making a sailor out of each individual.

It was interesting seeing the reaction to Trainee Day when we went to the 1988 Tall Ships Bicentennial event in Australia. Accolades, yes, but also sheer horror from people involved in running other youth development programmes. They said, 'You can't take those kids out and let them run the ship.' We said, 'What do you mean we can't? We do it all the time!'

In Hobart we disembarked the trainees who'd done the trans-Tasman voyage and then the next ones arrived by air from New Zealand. Totally green, not a sailor among them. The American ship *Eagle* was right ahead of us on the wharf and all these youngsters, 40 of them — just children, really — came walking down the wharf watched by hundreds of trainees off other ships, all in their twenties and in uniform, just looking in amazement at this young school group arriving to sail our ship.

The very next day we went out for a sail, about five or six hours at sea, and when we came back into the harbour we were able to sail the ship back alongside without the motor. That, I have to say, blew everybody away.

CHANGING LIVES

PAUL LEPPINGTON

Since he joined the Trust in 1975, Paul Leppington has served on the permanent crew as second mate, mate, permanent master and, in his current role, part-time senior master. Over this time he has played an important role in developing the Trust's educational programmes and operating and safety procedures. In 1998 he was one of the recipients of the Trust's inaugural Topgallant Award.

ONE CHARACTERISTIC of the Spirit of Adventure Trust is that, as well as any other youth development organisation and without any direct government help over thirty years, it has always moved forward and kept up with the times.

How have we learned to be proactive and not reactive? The people who teach us are our 'clients'; who else knows and understands teenagers better than other teenagers? Yet the safe operation of a ship is not a popular democracy but a caring autocracy where the master has the very highest good of his/her subjects at heart.

Young people are incredibly insightful; they are masters at spotting when someone is trying to 'mess with their heads' or has any ulterior motive. With this in mind, anyone who has half a chance of changing attitude or behaviour has to earn the right to do so. This is why we are prescriptive in the first few days when it is relatively easy, as the trainees will do anything you ask, happy to be helpful simply out of duty.

And if they will not follow? Then we must gain their confidence to allow us to lead, even into what they consider danger. Good leadership is not forced; it results from the chain reaction that has people feeding off each other's enthusiasm and from the energy that results.

The basic values that we display and want the trainees

Trainee at the wheel of *Spirit of New Zealand* with long-time volunteer mate John 'JR' Reeve, Hauraki Gulf, 1997.

to emulate are tested by time and are fundamental to our civilised society, summed up by the golden rule, 'Do unto others...' What can seem relatively inoffensive at home or school is magnified a thousand times in the crowded bunk room accommodation of our ship. It may be a boy's idea of great fun to have a mixed sleeping bunk room but a female trainee may have different ideas (or vice versa). Smelly socks are always a problem in youth, but a young man who never changes his socks for ten days is a real issue. Solutions lie largely in common sense. We separate the bravado from the foolish, real risk from perceived risk. For some it is possibly the first time that they are being taught values that mean anything at all. We are not concerned with a trainee's family background, but any dysfunction that exists in a family is eventually apparent to a greater or lesser degree, shown in behaviour problems on board.

The overview, the view of the end of the voyage, is sometimes unclear. However, we have to have the faith to complete our mission. We are a leading agent in developing the nation's youth, trusted by society to maintain traditions of encouraging and inspiring citizenship, leadership and, above all, teamwork.

To do this, we need to be very clear about our objectives and how we achieve them. We are not part of the NCEA

Trainees silhouetted against *Spirit of New Zealand's* yards. (Tessa Duder)

and certainly not attached to any school. The adults who sail as permanent crew or volunteers are sometimes trained teachers but more precisely they are life educators, with the responsibility of passing on those life skills to the selected 40 young people they are sailing with. The apparent ease with which we do it belies the fact that we are actually working at sea to change lives. We help young people define their own challenges, ones that they can relate to in the real everyday world and that eventually they can achieve.

How do we change people? From within, by giving them the time and attention that they may have never received before. Their time at sea is a time for change, helped if appropriate by adult and peer group intervention. Many of the students use this opportunity to initi-

ate often quite major changes in their lives, with the removal of their peer group, their habits, their parents, their school, their computer, their games machines, their music, their cellphones and their attitudes.

We can of course only make our assessments on what they present to us on arrival at the wharf — their apparent selves or the selves they would really *like* to be. We give them the chance to re-evaluate and reframe their persona without pressure from others. We have to break through this 'mask', remove it and rebuild it in a form that can be used by them in their real world — even if this may be only just a quick alter ego useful for their safety in times of crisis. If the only real development work we do is to give someone this safe place to go, then we have achieved our aim.

And how do you do all this in ten days? Yes, it's difficult, but the fact that we are not trying to change their whole life is important, and the shaping of any individual is 'one step at a time.' This may be simply to leave the deck to climb the mast, take greater personal responsibility for themselves or to fulfil the role of captain on Trainee Day.

The greatest single thing that *Spirit of New Zealand* passes on to trainees is its human relationship programme. Living with 39 other trainees you've never met before is the major catalyst for change. That we as an internationally much-respected sail and adventure training organisation have come to place greater emphasis on human relationships than on nautical education for its own sake is courageous and, from what we know of similar institutions, still unusual.

The general mandate that the late Lou Fisher gave to his Trust was for a *Spirit of Adventure* voyage to develop leadership, independence and community spirit through the medium of the sea. This has been further championed by his son, the present chairman Stephen Fisher, whose Trust Board steers the youth development programme, using a square-rig sailing ship as the vehicle to help develop and influence a young person's life.

The ability to have space and time to allow someone to develop a new way of seeing things is crucial to a voyage. This very subjective, warm fuzzy attitude has been the most difficult thing to describe and evaluate during the years the Trust has been running. Exactly what do we sell in this jar of goodies that is 'Spirit dust'?

It is to develop in trainees the ability to see the far horizon, to see the size of the seas. To figure out who they are personally and what might happen to them if they continue their current course of action in life. That they need the help of others to sail the vessel is very easily transferred to the need for others in life. To achieve, they must foster relationships and work as a team. Not a team in some trite 'team-building' exercise, but a real team, one that has to combine against the elements or literally go under.

Teamwork is not contrived in *Spirit of New Zealand*, not a set of building blocks on an imaginary river full of crocodiles. It is a fundamental life survival skill, dealing with a real weather forecast affecting a voyage between real places that has to be made by a definite date. It is this very real element that separates us from most other outdoor experiences. Our leadership development programme excels in its scope and popularity in the business marketplace because it is so real and practical. Most educators and teachers that I have come across would really love to be able to transfer their classroom to the ship and the Hauraki Gulf to progress their students. We often overlook this ingredient in our success: the Gulf and our proximity to it. The similar vessel to ours, STS *Leeuwin* in Western Australia, has to travel for days to the northwestern coast of Australia to get even an enclosed anchorage out of view of the city of Perth.

To be able to pass on information with relevance in an experiential format is priceless. The trainees pick up on it straight away. They are not graded, they are not examined and they will not get an assessment after the voyage. Simply they can be who they want to be, and at whatever level of academic or personal achievement they want to put forward. A sail will not go up or come down unless the right line is pulled; they don't need the name of the line, but they need to know which it is. After a while they quickly learn the nomenclature because it is simply quicker to name the line correctly than to call it 'that thingamajig'. The nautical vocabulary is very easy to learn when there is a need that is readily apparent. This is where experiential learning comes in: they see the need, and the tools to get the job done. There is no learning for learning's sake, no obscure connections. All they have to do is look up to the masts and the sails, and it's usually very obvious.

This and seasickness are the great levellers on the ship. The 'hands-on' learners and those who take a more intellectual approach learn to rely on each other's judgement. The left and right brainers are needed to overcome both the initial and follow-through problems. Once the sails are all going up and down well, then there's basic seamanship and the problems of navigation — then, who will cook and who will start the engines if they are needed?

So much has been made of Tomorrow's Schools that Today's have almost completely gone under, preoccupied that they are not being modern or fast-paced enough. The NCEA has affected the availability of students ready to

Old-style instruction, *Spirit of Adventure*. **Mate (and later master) Jim Revell is at the blackboard.**

come on the ship, but it has not changed the format of what we essentially do. Because there are fewer permanently scheduled outside examinations, schools are more flexible with internal assessments and course work. The scheme allows students with confidence and good negotiating skills to discuss with their teachers when a voyage is possible. The downside is that there are many schools (perhaps the majority) that have set examination and assessment periods. These used to be very clear and we could work around them, being able to schedule our refits in late October or early November. Now, to suit our ten-day voyage trainees, we schedule other voyages during that time, especially Spirit Trophy voyages for year ten (age 14-15) students.

The natural connection between the small boat sailors and the larger ship experience is not to be underrated. However, even the best small boat sailor is still mystified by the complexity of square rig and the sheer size of much of the ship's gear. Those with sailing experience can apply the same principles to *Spirit of New Zealand*, but in reali-

ty trainees start pretty much from scratch. There are no runners, bendy rigs, kevlar sails and fast-tacking duels. When the wind gets up, the sheer power of *Spirit of New Zealand* allows them to understand the dynamics of sailing a large square-rigged vessel. This is where the true character and ability of the trainee comes through, in how they translate any previous boating experience to the ship.

The typical voyage allows warm relationships and understanding among the crew and the trainees. That the trainees themselves are actually very close in physical proximity also allows and encourages them to be closer in their actual relational and personal space.

The programme by necessity compels trainees to be together, providing the camaraderie that channels and intensifies the experience. The laughter, tears, bravado and self-esteem crashes that are all part of a voyage come one after another. This has the effect of not allowing time for the person to grieve or become depressed following embarrassment or failure. Similarly, they rarely get time to feel elated by success before they have to work very hard to cover the last faux pas. The majority of these events are very minor and indeed are minimised by the crew, so that in competitive watch activities, no watch is allowed to get way ahead or way behind, and the emphasis is more on personal effort and responsibility than scores.

As a voyage progresses, trainees often choose to disclose information and stories to the group. This is one of the main reasons that the leading hands scheme is so successful. They act not as the meat in the sandwich but as an essential liaison between the crew and the trainees, truly the eyes and ears of the ship. If they are doing their job well, they are uniquely placed to hear the heartbeat of the trainees and the crew. The crew can then treat each trainee as an individual, well placed to deal with each issue as it arises, and to monitor and ideally curb poor behaviour before it develops.

How do today's trainees differ from those on the early voyages 30 years ago? Young people today are wired, switched on — not that they weren't in many ways 30 years ago — but the revolutions in media, electronics, education and understanding have changed teenagers for ever. It is not being reactionary to state that the naivety of youth has to a greater or lesser extent been lost. Young people grow up very quickly now; childhood rarely reaches beyond twelve or thirteen. By childhood I mean innocence, playing for hours in the outdoors rather than saving a planet invaded by aliens, being able to have fun without stimulants and artificial means.

Thirty years ago teenagers had a more rounded education in life, where basic values were intrinsic and did not have to be introduced, even justified and defended by the ship's crew. Certain things were taken for granted, like respect and looking after each other. Nowadays, in rare cases, we have to explain that for a watch to complete a task they will all have to look after one other. What was once seen as common sense seems today to be a rarer commodity and has to be pointed out far more frequently.

There have always been boisterous, rebellious youth in every age, but contemporary trainees with a negative attitude will challenge you over their 'rights' and disrupt the whole voyage, given half a chance. Sometimes these negative attitudes are so ingrained that these trainees cannot be brought around and reintegrated into the group. In a few cases we are finding removal from the voyage is the only recourse open to the crew. Even that has changed, in that the threat or actuality of being sent home from the ship is no longer seen as a disgrace, but a personal trophy showing how they were 'above the system'.

An activity dubbed the 'Amazon' was started very early in the Trust's programme and is still a winner. It consists of getting up before dawn and launching the small boats. You row up a river, getting as far up as you can, then cook breakfast on a campfire while the sun comes up and the birds sing. Then you row back to the ship with trainees who are usually very animated and crew very happy. However, the timing is critical: light the campfire and cook the barbecue too soon and you have trainees sitting around wanting their ghetto blasters; just right, and you have a group reluctant to stop their own singing and return to the ship.

As we slow down their pace long enough to see the stars and the sunrise, they get a glimpse of a reality that is not based on being fast, sophisticated and cool, but connected

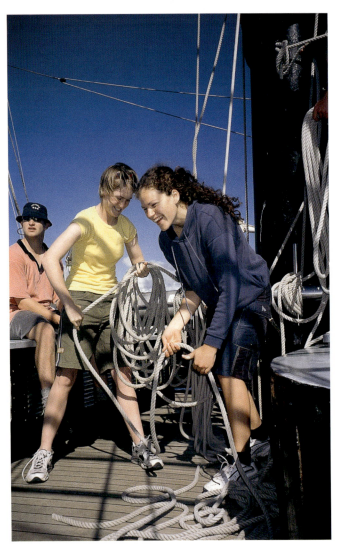

Coiling ropes on board *Spirit of New Zealand*, **Hauraki Gulf, 1997.**

to nature and a rhythm of life quite different from the 'jet-stream' culture in which they normally live. This is an age when many young men and women have to deal early with the harsh realities of life, like budgets, meals and shelter, rather than school life and career choices. The information age does not necessarily bring wisdom, and character is rarely found in a 'Gameboy'. We have the time to reintroduce young people to laughter and natural fun, shared in a safe place by adults who are good role models and are not perceived as perpetrators of 'the system'.

HARD DECISIONS

TESSA DUDER

FACTS ABOUT SHIPS are easily chronicled: *Spirit of Adventure* was conceived in 1970, launched in December 1973, and undertook her first youth voyage in January 1974. She was sold in 1997. Fundraising for *Spirit of New Zealand* began in June 1982; costing around $3.5 m, she was commissioned in July 1986. Her first youth voyage followed in September 1986.

Behind the bare facts, however, lies a great deal of decision- and policy-making, by a small board of appointed trustees and outside advisers. Building and running a sailing ship is a costly exercise requiring commitment, stamina and huge resources of money and people; operating two at the same time, which the Trust did for eleven years, is tantamount to running a small shipping line. Weave through this a youth development programme and the total picture becomes complex.

It is easy to chart the growth of confidence during the 1970s. *Spirit of Adventure* began plying the Hauraki Gulf, expanded to Whangarei and Tauranga, and in 1979 was ready for her first southern voyage, to Wellington and the Marlborough Sounds. These southern trips became annual: in 1981 she sailed for the first time to the deep south, Bluff and Stewart Island, and in 1984 completed her first circumnavigation. By the end of 1985, the 'white ship' was estimated to have sailed 95,000 miles.

The decision to build a second ship was taken after much Board discussion relating to the most appropriate way to extend the Trust's operations, counter complacency and cater for a greater number of young New Zealanders. The Trust was at the time managing at slightly better than a break-even point; a vessel with a larger carrying capacity would be more economic to operate. The decision was also influenced by growing confidence in taking 20-odd teenagers safely to sea on a square-rigger, and the strengthening demand for berths. The *Spirit* experience was now embedded in secondary school culture as a desirable and worthwhile opportunity, and the Trust Board wanted a ship that would be seen as a fully national (not Auckland) enterprise.

Eighteen months of planning and discussion had already taken place before the *Spirit of New Zealand* fundraising campaign was announced in June 1982. Plans for the new vessel were drawn up by Ewbank Brooke and a campaign team was employed and established in the chairman's office. The late Sir Peter Blake lent his name and energy to some of the campaign initiatives. Informed by the chairman, while reviewing the new ship drawings during a visit to *Spirit of Adventure*, that the Trust planned to replace her with a larger vessel, the Duke of Edinburgh replied briskly, 'Be damned you're going to sell her. You're going to operate two!'

With sufficient funds in hand, a contract was let to begin building *Spirit of New Zealand* on a 'continuation funds permitting' basis. With two ships operating, new challenges appeared. Friendly rivalry developed between 'white' and 'black' ships and close to 1800 trainees could now sail each year. The next ten years, however, were times of political, social and educational upheaval, including the sharemarket crash and subsequent major recession. Two ships more or less

Sir Peter Blake (back row, third from left) with Stephen Fisher (far right) and early members of the campaign team set up in 1982 to raise funds for *Spirit of New Zealand*.

simultaneously at sea, requiring around 18 crew and increased office staff to provide berths for a total of 65 trainees every two weeks, put huge and growing strain on the operation.

Although the Trust's public profile was high, by early 1997 this strain was becoming untenable. Despite strenuous efforts, and because the Trust Board declined to pass the costs of servicing its overdraft and maintenance of an ageing ship on to the trainee fees, the financial outlook was unacceptable. Amid growing competition from school-run adventure programmes, it had become increasingly difficult for office staff to ensure the ships sailed full, especially with male trainees. Volunteer input was still adequate, but lacked the depth it had enjoyed previously.

In February, after six months of agonising and anticipating that many of its devoted volunteers would have difficulty understanding the reasoning, the Trust Board accepted that *Spirit of Adventure*'s economic life as a sail-training ship was at an end, and reluctantly decided to sell her while she was still in reasonably good shape. Her new owners were to be Captain Cook Cruises, operating out of Nadi, Fiji. Under the command of trustee and volunteer master Captain Jim Varney, she sailed out of the

The decommissioning of *Spirit of Adventure* on the Waitemata Harbour, 17 August 1997. (John Newsham)

Waitemata Harbour for the last time in September 1997.

Since that date, *Spirit of New Zealand* has plied New Zealand's coastal waters alone. The decision to sell the 'white ship' has proved a prudent one: in the five years since, the financial situation has improved and stabilised, the demand for berths is again buoyant and the system of

THE SPIRIT TROPHY VOYAGES

OCTOBER and November are traditionally quiet months for *Spirit of New Zealand*. At this time of year a large proportion of the 'target market' is bent over its collective books, studying for exams.

So how to make the most of the seasonal lull? One long-used solution has been to schedule *Spirit*'s annual refit for this time of year. A second, since 1998, has been the five-day Spirit Trophy voyages for fourth form (year ten) students.

Competing for the Spirit Trophy, teams from four schools participate in a mix of competitive activities designed to encourage teamwork in and on the water. Each team of ten students is accompanied by a teacher in the role of leading hand.

The Trophy's highly competitive voyages provide an interesting contrast to the Trust's core business, the ten-day voyages, where the competitive element is less marked and more emphasis is placed on personal development.

According to CEO John Lister, the success of the Trophy voyages has been phenomenal, with more than 60 schools applying for 24 team places in the 2003 programme. Feedback from teachers praises 'an excellent learning experience for students in group skills, leadership and confidence building,' and states that 'students extended themselves, met new challenges, people, environment, and took themselves out of their comfort zone.'

Further benefits are the likely return of many of these 14-year-olds as ten-day trainees and an influential first-hand experience for teachers.

two alternating crews ensures less fatigue and greater stability amongst the sea-going staff. The Trust has settled into its core business of ten-day youth development voyages around northern waters, augmented by regular Disabled, Leader Manager, Spirit Trophy and southern voyages. It also had the resources to take advantage of the fundraising opportunities presented by two Louis Vuitton/America's Cup campaigns in 2000 and 2003.

With an eye to the longevity of the Trust's activities and continuance of the programme, in 1992 the Trust Board set up the Spirit of Adventure Foundation. Ongoing financial commitments were secured from a new category of Life Members, and investments included the establishment of a 90-hectare forest near Lake Rotoehu, not far from Rotorua. A joint venture between the Spirit of Adventure Trust and Fletcher Forests, the forest will be reaching maturity at about the time that the Trust Board will be considering the design and funding for a new vessel to replace *Spirit of New Zealand*. On today's prices the capital requirement could be close to $20 million.

After fifteen years, *Spirit of New Zealand* underwent a $500,000 major half-life refit in 2001 and is predicted to reach the end of her economic life after thirty years at sea, around 2016.

FUNDING

SINCE ITS INCEPTION in 1973, one of the basic aims of the Spirit of Adventure Trust Board has been that a ten-day youth development voyage should be available to all young New Zealanders, regardless of their financial background. The Board decided then that a standard trainee fee would include travel from any place in New Zealand. This policy has remained unchanged — even at the cost to the Trust of shouldering around one-third of the real trainee fee and needing to fundraise relentlessly, just to cover operating costs, at the rate of about $10,000 per week, or half a million dollars annually.

In practical terms, this policy has had two effects. First, it has meant that the Trust has kept the fees it charges its trainees as low as possible. (In 2003 voyage fees are $900 per trainee, approximately 60 percent of true cost.) Keeping fees low has forced the Trust to look to sources other than fees for the extra funding needed to run its operations. These sources take two forms: commercial public sailings (e.g. day sails and adult weekends) and charitable fundraising. It amounts to a lot of money in anyone's book, and the Trust is extremely grateful to the many organisations and individuals whose generous support — financial and in kind — enables it to keep running.

Secondly, this policy has led to the Trust putting in place special programmes to subsidise the fees of young people who could not otherwise afford a voyage. In 1989 it established the John Wallace McKenzie Memorial Trust for this purpose, in memory of its late deputy chairman. This programme received a further boost in 2001, following a generous donation from the Team New Zealand 2000 Trust, at the instigation of Sir Peter Blake. By amalgamating the two sources of funds, the Trust established a new trust known as the Spirit of Adventure Trust Team New Zealand Scholarship.

The new trust has funds of around $350,000. Each year it can help about 60 young people who would not otherwise be able to make a voyage, around two trainees per voyage. There is no stigma attached to receiving this funding. Fellow trainees are unaware that a trainee has received funding unless the trainee chooses to tell them.

The Spirit of Adventure Trust Team New Zealand Scholarship does not pay the full amount of a trainee's fees. The Trust is keen that all young people, whether on subsidised passages or not, use their initiative to pay for their fees. It encourages them to approach other organisations for funding, such as service clubs and community licensing trusts, and to raise money from their own efforts. There are many heart-warming stories. One member of the operations office recalls a young girl from Northland who was so desperate to go on a voyage that she raised her full $900 contribution from baby-sitting.

PART 2

TEAMWORK

THE VOYAGERS CLUB

RON BIRD

Ron Bird, one of the Trust's first permanent engineers, is also one of its most enduring characters — as volunteer engineer, mate, archivist and, in 1975, founder and tireless promoter of the Voyagers Club. Over thirty years he has maintained a wide network of former trainees with whom he sailed or whom he met in the first ten years of the club, when Voyagers were involved in refits, fundraising, boat shows and telethons.

Ron Bird

THE VERY FIRST VOYAGERS meeting was held one wet night in September 1975, in the tin shed on Marsden Wharf. Trustees John Duder and Captain Barry Thompson were among the group that were meeting mainly to get a committee up and running.

The Voyagers Club name was already decided by then, probably by the then operations director James Lennox-King, who had prepared certificates stating that the trainee had completed a voyage and was now qualified to be a member of the Voyagers Club. So there was no official launch to the Voyagers Club, it just happened.

When I came along as watch officer for the first girls' voyage in June 1974 there was no structure, nothing, just these certificates. By September 1975 we decided there were sufficient ex-trainees — going on for a thousand — to put together a reunion ball, not exactly as the launch of the club but as a first major function. It was held on 14 August 1976, at the West End Rowing Club, when Lou Fisher came and spoke to the assembled company of about 150. It was quite a dressy affair.

At that stage, the concept of returning to sail on the ship as leading hands hadn't arisen. The focus was simply, we had a great time, let's keep that rolling. The club soon showed its strength by helping with the November refits. One year on the Vos and Brijs slip, Voyagers put in 4000 person hours, with key members like Tony Bryant, Grey Hutchinson and Peter Kane working all hours and doing terrible jobs like chipping out the anchor locker.

There was no ulterior motive in the formation of the club, and for many years no carrot, e.g. the chance to get back on the ship. The only opportunity then, until the leading hands scheme was developed in 1979, was the annual Voyagers Club day sail after refit.

After that first ball, they got stuck into refits, and the group of boys selected to sail on the fine *Bounty* replica in 1979 was given a wonderful insight into traditional seafaring. Afterwards, when they wanted to return on *Spirit of Adventure*, it was quite difficult to pull those young people back in and say, for instance, this is not *Bounty* and we wear safety harnesses on *Spirit*. Then we had the Telethons, doing mad things like towing models of the ship up and down

Queen Street asking for money, and doing time at the boat shows, standing in draughty corridors for days on end in the old Greenlane Events Centre. And there were fundraising exercises, for projects like the beautiful carved wooden dolphins placed on either side of *Spirit of Adventure*'s bow. There was a great sense of pride in those early years, noticeable for example in guarding their sole right to wear their trainee and Voyagers Club T-shirts.

So what makes young people come back as Voyagers? I can only go back to the effect on me as an adult. I can't describe the long-term effect, but I know it was profound, and I still think back to that first trip, working with young people, shoulder to shoulder in close confines, sharing all sorts of wonderful experiences, the camaraderie. It was a voyage on the edge of a cyclone, and we had people calling the ship, asking if the girls were all right, only to be told they're dancing round the foremast at present. We were quite happy, and the rough weather was part of it.

The *Spirit* experience is increasingly important as the organisation fosters team-building, when these days the focus is very much on everyone looking after themselves, with fewer people joining organisations, unlike earlier times when there was compulsory military service. It was predicted ten or so years ago that group activities would be weakened by the 'do your own thing' culture. And it's a tribute to what happens on the ship that, unlike organisations like Scouts which have many years to help young people, we can turn them around in just ten days. That's quite something. We do have famous ex-trainees, but in my view that is not the focus — rather, we quietly work away at the average Kiwi youngster, sometimes those who've had problems with the courts or maybe just the one who was struggling, and the *Spirit* experience helps them get to where ordinary people are.

I've lost count of how many handkerchiefs I've lost at the ends of voyages. Some you never see again, some come back washed in the mail, such is that involvement and enthusiasm, that sense of belonging.

Now, besides providing leading hands for each voyage, possibly the best thing Voyagers are doing is going and talking to schools in their area. There's nothing better than having a youngster talking about their trip and sharing their enthusiasm.

Voyagers Club president Kim Patterson presents Prime Minister David Lange with a *Spirit of Adventure* plaque following the unveiling of the dolphins on the bow of *Spirit of Adventure* in 1984. The dolphins were a gift from the Voyagers Club.

VOYAGERS ARE SPECIAL PEOPLE

MIKE TAYLOR

Mike Taylor grew up on Auckland's North Shore but now lives on Waiheke Island, running a property development company and yacht charter business. His extensive sailing experience ranges from P-class to family cruising on his own 37-foot yacht. After some years practising law, he took time off to drive through Africa, and on his return became involved with the Spirit of Adventure Trust, with special interest in the Voyagers Club and the schools' speaking programme.

THE VOYAGERS CLUB has its own president, national executive committee and branches in all the main cities. It also has smaller clusters in pockets all over New Zealand. The Voyagers' 25th anniversary ball in 1999 was an impressive milestone marking a significant period of survival, laughter and shared memories from the early voyages on *Adventure* to recent voyages on *New Zealand*. The Voyagers Club arranges regular annual skiing trips away, in both the North and South Islands, camping trips to the Kai-iwi lakes near Dargaville, and many other events to enable Voyagers from different parts of New Zealand to get together.

Delivering something back to the Spirit organisation is key to the existence of the Voyagers, and alongside the reliable supply of leading hands, the Voyagers regularly show that, when called upon, they can deliver. The best recent example of this was the half-life refit of *Spirit of New Zealand* in 2000. Within a week of a call from CEO John Lister, the Voyagers Club took on the responsibility of raising $3,000 needed for a replacement royal sail, the proud sail set from the ship's highest yard. From Northland to the lower South Island, Voyagers swung into action with all manner of fundraising, including sausage sizzles and selling raffle tickets and Spirit pens, quickly raising over twice the target amount.

The formal unveiling of the brilliantly white new royal took place on board *Spirit of New Zealand* on the Saturday night of the first dedicated Voyagers training weekend in 2001. To the sound of ceremonial bagpipes, the spot-lit sail was slowly set from the deck and sixty uniformed Voyagers celebrated their club's achievement. The training weekend itself, made possible by a Lottery Board grant for training as part of the International Year of the Volunteer, brought together Voyagers from all over New Zealand for a weekend's valuable training from permanent and volunteer crew on all aspects of being a Voyager. We even managed a morning swim (at the local swimming baths rather than alongside the wharf).

The inaugural training weekend was hailed by all involved as a huge success. Many of the permanent and volunteer crew gave up their time to deliver an excellent package of information, including their own expectations of leading hands.

Some of the most difficult aspects of being a leading hand were tackled, such as trying to quieten down 20 excited trainees in the accommodation at 11pm after an exhilarating day. It was a good opportunity for Voyagers to ask questions, and take the ship sailing for that all too rare chance to get hands-on practice.

One important tradition of the Voyagers Club is the annual Easter conference, held alternately in the North and South Islands and providing a chance for Voyagers to meet old friends and make new ones. Organised by the national committee of the day, these conferences involve much fun and laughter alongside the formal election of the coming year's national committee. Over the past few years a mystery guest speaker has added some intrigue, including mountaineer Peter Hillary and Cameron Appleton, Team New Zealand's back-up helmsman for the 2003 defence.

In 2000 and 2001, the Voyagers Club decided to identify and reassess its reason for existence. This was not an easy question, but after much discussion, the national committee settled upon a clear purpose, later accepted by the club itself: 'To create opportunities for self-development and to make a positive difference to the Spirit of Adventure Trust and to the community.' The club is also very much about having fun, and enjoying the company of others who have been through the same experience.

Members of the Voyagers Club in uniform for the presentation to the Trust Board of the new royal sail, 2002.
(Tessa Duder)

Spirit of New Zealand (left) takes part in the millennium celebrations, Gisborne, 1 January 2000. (Dominion Post)

SPIRIT SONNET

Our sleek, black ship with sails so high,
Oft sighted round New Zealand's rugged shore,
As, like a distant vision, you sail by
And o'er the horizon then are seen no more.
The landsman cannot know viewed from afar
The power of wind in sails that makes you heel,
The lofty masts and yard that catch a star
To guide the midnight helmsman at the wheel.
The brave young hearts who tend you as your crew,
Anxious at first, uncertain and untried.
You reveal the strengths and truths they never knew,
Teamwork, tolerance, courage, friendship, pride.
Could you but speak what magic tales you'd tell
Of young lives changed by your miraculous spell.

JOYCE LAVENDER

As a part of its ongoing commitment to the Spirit of Adventure Trust, the Voyagers Club has always provided leading hands for the ships, and even takes responsibility for rostering them on. This is no small task for people under 25 (and often under 20) to undertake. The rosterer comes under immense pressure to find people, especially for the unpopular times (such as mid-winter, and in the lead-up to exams). I have always been impressed with the recognition of the seriousness of this role by successive rosterers and the Voyagers Club in general. There is a reliable and sometimes stunning ability to deal with difficulties and deliver. Despite panics and last-minute changes, the rosterer always comes through!

The year 2000 also saw the introduction of the Topsail Award —a special award instituted by the Trust Board to honour an outstanding Voyager who has given three or more years' excellent service to the Trust and the Voyagers

Club. There can be up to three awards made each year, and it is a valuable recognition of an individual Voyager's contribution at local or national level.

All things go in cycles, and this is true of the Voyagers Club. Total membership fluctuates, but it is fair to say that the club is re-establishing itself nationally, focused on building its membership into a strong national identity that can deliver something of real value to its members, the Spirit organisation and to the general community.

I believe that what we as an organisation do on board the ship is magic. It's about sailing, but so much more. We open eyes, doors, worlds and can change lives. I believe that every trainee steps off the ship after ten days with something special that they did not have when they stepped aboard. Yes, new friends, but more than that. So often it is a belief that they can do things that might seem at first sight out of reach.

I've seen someone's life change in thirty seconds. She was 16, and afraid of heights. Actually, there was a lot on the ship that frightened her. On day three it was our watch on the square sails at midships, and thus with the job of climbing aloft. At the bottom of the first futtocks, about a third of the way up the mast and about ten metres off the deck, there is a small climb outwards at an angle of around 30 degrees. This is the most daunting part of the climb to many people — and it certainly was to this trainee. Although tethered with a safety harness, she began to shake with fear. Frozen, with both hands reaching at full stretch up to the platform that represents safety, she quietly said she couldn't hold on and was going to fall. Tears began rolling down her face, and her grip began to slide from the metal rigging. I climbed out and gently put a hand squarely behind her back, and said, 'You are not going to fall, but you have a choice to make. You can climb up here, and I know you can do that — or you can go down now. There's no shame in going down — you've done well to get to here, but I know you can climb up there.' I looked at her and asked, 'What would you like to do?' She said she would try.

Slowly she moved one foot, then the other. Moving her white knuckle grasp slightly higher, with fast grabs at the rigging, she inched her way up. She began to get some momentum, and within seconds, swung herself on to the platform. She had an energetic shine in her eyes, and although still a little shaky, she was fizzing inside.

From that time onwards in the voyage, this trainee was one of the first volunteers for anything going. She was simply not the same person. I believe she stepped off the ship at the end of that voyage with an inner belief in herself that she didn't have when she stepped aboard at the start. When she next encounters a major challenge in her life, and her first reaction is 'I cannot do this', perhaps she will try anyway. Perhaps she will surmount the challenge despite the fear and doubt — after all, she has done so once before.

I think there are three types of opportunities for trainees on a ten-day voyage. First there are 'inherent opportunities' — those presented by the unique environ-

CAPTAIN UNDERPANTS

The weather often dictates the day's activities on Spirit. Every wise captain respects the elements and Captain Jim Dilley is no exception. Jim has a particular love of weather charts and a real gift for conveying complex, scientific information in a fun and comprehensive way. On this voyage, his 'girl fronts' and 'boy fronts' soon resulted in a new nickname: 'Captain Underpants'.

Captain Jim truly earned this title on one of the last days of the voyage when he appeared on deck in thermals, undies, a cape and mask. He was fulfilling a trainee request and honouring it in true style! Captain Underpants proceeded to swing off the deck and somersault dramatically into the ocean. The trainees roared. He had their full respect.

ANNETTE CULPAN
Volunteer crew

ment of the ship itself. These are largely inescapable opportunities and are delivered to every trainee aboard. They include the chance to learn and experience sailing a square-rigger, to face a challenge and to meet new people.

Then there are those opportunities presented on a silver platter — opportunities that all trainees are led through during the voyage but which not all take up, such as the chance to try out leading your watch and to learn to be compassionate and supportive.

Finally, there are hidden opportunities. These are chances to take initiative and shine, to look about you, take in what is happening and really make something of the voyage.

Whatever opportunities a trainee takes up, there are major benefits. For some, particularly trainees who arrive at the ship with a low self-esteem, meeting the inherent opportunities will be a great achievement. For others, it is a unique opportunity to stand out from the crowd.

When two Voyagers meet, there is an instant understanding of the voyage and those special moments. You can see it in the smiles and feel it in their energy. This is what the trainees all share as they come to the end of their voyage. This is the magnetic adhesive quality of the Voyagers Club.

Wellington Voyagers enjoy a day sail on *Spirit of New Zealand,* **December 1999.**
(Veronica Gailitis)

WHY THE VOYAGERS CLUB WORKS

ADRIENNE WELCH

Adrienne Welch, of Auckland, was one of the first women to win the coveted Topgallant Award, given by the Spirit of Adventure Trust Board to mark more than 10 years' distinguished service to the Trust. Over more than 20 years, she has been liaison officer for the Voyagers Club and for the overall community of volunteers nationally, as well as Wellington port contact and chairperson of the Wellington Regional Association. A high school geography teacher, she is now the Trust's honorary adviser on educational matters and a member of the magazine editorial team.

WHAT IS THE SECRET of the Voyagers Club's success? How does it operate and what do its members gain from being involved?

These are questions of interest to me as I have an unusual perspective on the Voyagers Club, having been 'of it but not in it' for nearly five years from 1983 to the end of 1987 when I was (officially anyway) their employee. My title was liaison officer for the national executive of the Voyagers Club, although this hardly describes my role. The Voyagers had more colloquial descriptions such as 'the Club's resident grown-up', 'the old girl', 'mother hen' and 'granny' (as long as I wasn't too close) and more colourful expressions that I wasn't meant to know about.

The role evolved over time and became a sort of one-person Citizens Advice Bureau and advisory service. I liaised with anyone they wanted me to, acted as a clearing-house for files, information and addresses, and was required at times to maintain continuity when individuals moved, took over or left a position. I even had occasion to track down office-holders and extract club files when life's circumstances (usually love!) suddenly changed their priorities. All of which can be summarised by saying I was employed to help them run the club themselves.

The first Annual General Meeting of the Voyagers Club was in 1979. There are currently 15 branches and the national executive. From time to time an area will go into recess, but they come bouncing back again when a new lot of enthusiastic, inspired teenagers arrives home after their ten-day trainee trip.

The development of the Volunteer Crew Association and then regional associations in the mid-1980s has helped give them back-up support in the various parts of New Zealand — but the Voyagers Club branches were there first. The wonder to me is not that occasionally parts of the club are not as strong or efficient as some people (usually the staff of the operations office and Trust Board) would like, but that it has been continuous and the national executive has never gone into recess.

The motivation for many to get involved is a desire to get back on that beautiful

NOT QUITE WHAT I MEANT!

The watch leader, keen to inspire her team with the wonders of navigation, had spent some time that morning explaining chart symbols and their uses. Later the same day, on a raft approaching Tonga Island in the Abel Tasman National Park, they passed close to a partially submerged rock.

'Hey look,' she said. 'Over there's a neat example of a rock awash. Just what we were talking about this morning.'

The trainee beside her seemed puzzled.

The watch leader pointed again. 'Over there. Right behind you.'

'Yes,' said the trainee. 'I can see the rock. But where's the symbol?'

NICKY JENKINS
Volunteer crew

Trainee at the wheel of *Spirit of New Zealand*.

square-rigger again. The bonding experiences so often encountered on their own trip can also be a positive influence. What they end up with — as well as the chance to sail on that magic ship again — is a network of friends and acquaintances, invaluable experience running a voluntary community organisation and free accommodation all over the country that continues for many years after they leave the club. And the only thing these people had in common was the opportunity to spend ten days (or in special circumstances five days) floating around the seas of New Zealand in an old-fashioned sailing ship.

The very definition of a youth club means that the individuals move through and move on when they feel they have 'outgrown' the club. The Voyagers range from 15 to 25, although most active participants would be in the middle age range.

Ex-trainees tend to start off with the local group where social and fundraising activities are organised. Leaving school, when the known patterns of their life change, can be a trigger point for more active involvement. If the ship visits the local port this gives many a chance to crew again for day sails. When they reach 18 they are eligible to be a leading hand for a ten-day sail.

Branches run meetings, organise social occasions and fundraising activities and most produce a newsletter. For those who wish to sail again on the ship, training courses are held with the local volunteer crew. If they stay on, they may become more active at a national level, which involves producing a national newsletter, organising a national conference each year and rostering leading hands for every ten-day voyage.

This pattern of involvement may not seem unusual except when you start considering some of the characteristics of this age group and the circumstances in which they meet and operate their club. All these factors make this venture unlikely to succeed:

- The fact that the only time they have met one another is on their trip. Often they will be the only student from their district so they have no direct connections with members in their own region.
- The huge difference in maturity between the new school leavers and the young trained adult (the ugly duckling to swan process) which often takes place in less time than they spent at secondary school.
- Their stage in life: when they leave school there are dramas and crises involved in moving from home to flats, moving from home town to wherever and learning to live with people other than their family. Not to mention the agonies of the first experiences falling in and out of love.
- The sense of freedom and independence they feel as they leave school and have a chance to flex their muscles without parents, teachers or trainers 'in charge', probably for the first time. This is often manifested by there being little or no sense of time being important. The young people are always running late and 'it doesn't matter'.
- The directness with which they tackle each other — a certain lack of tact and discretion that can cause major fallout.
- The lack of ready money as many are on training courses.
- The geographical spread and distances in New Zealand.

So why does it work?

First, the absolute acceptance of everyone without question. You don't have to be good at anything, a leader or an achiever. You only have to have done a voyage. Despite their directness they still accept the other person's right to be part of the group. The strong bonding from the trainee trip gets transferred to club members once the initial contact has been made in the home region.

Then, the camaraderie and loyalty which is an outcome of the way the trainee programme is run. This encourages a supportive atmosphere with the group working as a team with their peers, help-

Editorial team for the *Spirit of Adventure* magazine: Tessa Duder, John Lister, Adrienne Welch. Absent: Kate Thompson.

Voyagers on board *Spirit of New Zealand* during the America's Cup regatta 2003 sport their red socks in support of Team New Zealand.
(Tessa Duder)

ing each other and sharing decisions. All credit is due to the vision of the founding Trust Board in setting up a culture and programme very different from the school environment trainees come from. A related advantage here is that the Voyagers are of an age group that has boundless energy and a great sense of fun.

For the Trust Board and the future of its youth development programme 'through the medium of the sea', a visibly strong and active youth club is the 'proof of the pudding'. Adult members in all areas are prepared to support the club, creating respect and easy relationships between all age groups from 15 to 80 plus, a truly egalitarian New Zealand way.

However, I have observed that the Voyagers are fiercely protective of their autonomy and independence and always suspicious that there might be a takeover by the other groups who they see as 'authority' (anyone over 25!). I grew to respect this, as they are breaking out from the authoritarian systems of school (and in some cases home).

When the Trust Board ran two ships from 1986 to 1997, the number of trainees produced every fortnight rose from 24 to 66. This required streamlining many systems right throughout the Voyagers Club: membership fees, newsletters, relationships between different interest groups, training and, last but not least, communication.

Communication is the most persistent ongoing challenge. Since the start of the Voyagers Club we have seen snail mail (handwritten or typed) and carbon copies replaced by photocopiers, fax machines, email and electronic news groups. Basic telephones (not even cordless) with expensive toll calls have developed into cheap toll calls, with cellphones and texting popular. The advantage for the Voyagers Club is that their age group is usually the first to pick up on new technology.

In the end though, it's still the human factor that makes the difference — the individuals charged with the ongoing task of making and keeping contact with current and potential members.

What have I learnt from the Voyagers Club about youth groups? Despite some well-meaning folks' assertion that bigger is better, I don't think it's necessarily so. The development of individuals — through camaraderie, commitment and confidence — is the club's principal achievement. Sometimes that development extends beyond their wildest dreams, taking that initial experience at sea as a trainee on to another level altogether. The Voyagers Club is simply a vehicle enabling many of the original trainees to keep on developing those qualities.

VOYAGES FOR DISABLED TRAINEES

JOYCE LAVENDER

Following a visit from Fred Kilgour of Britain's Jubilee Sailing Trust (then raising money for the Lord Nelson, *a purpose-built square-rigger for the disabled) Joyce Lavender approached the Spirit of Adventure Trust in 1983 to propose special voyages for disabled trainees. Nearly twenty years later she handed over her role as the Trust's disabled voyage co-ordinator to Sonya Thursby, and was appointed the Trust's honorary adviser (disabilities).*

VOYAGE 421HC in March 1984 was the first voyage on *Spirit of Adventure* for young people with physical disabilities. Hitherto it had been considered that these youngsters could not participate in what were perceived 'risk' activities; they were excluded from school camps and outdoor recreation programmes and set apart from their peers, leading to a sense of isolation and loneliness.

In the 1970s attitudes began to change, thanks to more enlightened thinking and a move towards including people with disabilities in the mainstream of community activities. As national recreation director of the New Zealand Crippled Children's Society (now renamed New Zealand CCS), I had been involved in the late seventies in setting up and establishing courses for disabled youngsters at the Hillary Outdoor Pursuits Centre in Turangi and at Outward Bound. The Spirit of Adventure Trust seemed the next obvious challenge.

This proved a little more difficult, as safety at sea was of paramount importance and the old adage of 'one hand for yourself and one hand for the ship' was a little hard to apply when some youngsters only had one good hand anyway. However, with the enthusiastic support of Captain Nick Hylton, Captain Barry Thompson and Tessa Duder, the first trial three-day voyage took place out of Wellington on Friday 9 March 1984, involving twelve trainees with a range of disabilities and twelve Voyager buddies (to provide those extra hands and general support) drawn from all over New Zealand. The voyage was sponsored by the Tasman Pulp and Paper Company, and attracted huge media coverage with TV cameramen and reporters swarming all over the ship, but the resulting publicity was most valuable in emphasising the abilities of these youngsters.

The original intention was to sail across Cook Strait to the Marlborough Sounds, but Wellington's famous blustery weather kept us within harbour limits, although still providing an exciting challenge for the new trainees. The voyage was deemed a great success. The trainees did amazingly well in accepting the unaccustomed responsibilities of sailing the ship, hoisting the sails, steering and keeping anchor watch at night with the initial aid and support of their buddies. They responded willingly and enthusiastically to the new challenge, encouraged by the

Trainee Hona Taiapa was in a coma and then a wheelchair for a time, after suffering a stroke in 1999. He wrote this letter to his sponsor with the help of his buddy on the voyage.

Thanks for your sponsorship. I would just like to say that I had a massively enjoyable time. I have done things I thought I could never do, such as socialising and getting to know other people with disabilities, and the best opportunity I had was to climb the square sails mast. Things will never be the same again for me, as this experience has helped me to come to terms with my problem and given me back my confidence in myself. This is no exaggeration and I sincerely mean this. This voyage will help me face the future in a more positive way.

Hona wrote also to Joyce Lavender:
That voyage on the *Spirit* changed my whole look on life. I'm confident now, and I know how to talk and I am not ashamed to say what I want said. My family has noticed a big change in me, so my life is looking very good.
PS Thank you for opening my world for me.

Disabled trainee Charlie Joseph from Wanganui at the helm of *Spirit of New Zealand*, Voyage 342H, May 2001. (Joyce Lavender)

competent and kindly leadership of Nick Hylton as master.

The trainees included those with physical disabilities and others who had visual and hearing impairments. In the 1990s the ratio of trainees to buddies was reduced to 30:12 as many trainees needed general support rather than a one-to-one buddy. This revised policy has allowed us to take more trainees and they in turn have had to take on more responsibility and work, presenting them with greater challenges.

Since that first experience, an annual voyage has been established on the ship's schedule, and now some five hundred youngsters with disabilities have taken part in five-day voyages on *Spirit of New Zealand* and, until 1997, *Spirit of Adventure*.

The trainees arrive on board shy, hesitant and a little apprehensive of the challenge ahead, but leave the ship at the end of a voyage walking tall and proud of their personal and team achievements, with enhanced self-confidence as a result of their adventure, and with many new friends to keep in touch with. They have great stories to tell family and friends when they arrive home — for many, the voyage is the highlight of their young lives.

As with every able-bodied voyage, there are many stories of achievement and success. On the first voyage, one girl who was totally blind climbed to the very top of *Spirit of Adventure's* mast, to the amazement of her fellow trainees and buddies. I recall one young woman who had lost her sight in a road accident, having just returned from a frantic water fun fight in the rubber dinghies, standing dripping on the deck and saying, 'I didn't know you could have so much fun without being a brat.' She admitted she had been wild and irresponsible before her accident but the voyage had given her a whole new outlook on life.

Another young trainee arrived on board terrified and in tears at having to negotiate the ten or so steps down to the lower deck. At the end of the voyage she cheerfully allowed herself to be hoisted in a bosun's chair to the top of the mast and, with the encouragement of her buddy, stepped out on to the footrope to make her way along the highest yardarm. What an incredible feat of courage.

Then there was a young man with cerebral palsy who, in a letter after the voyage, said, 'My mum says I have grown five years in five days.'

There is no doubt that these voyages have had an immense influence on the lives of many disabled young people over the years, and recognition must go to the Spirit of Adventure Trust for their commitment to the concept of equal opportunity for all young people. The permanent crew also adapted the sailing programme and provided encouragement, while the watch leaders and Voyager buddies have willingly volunteered their time, skills and friendship in support of the trainees and have themselves gained much from the experience.

Financial support needs also to be acknowledged, from the Half Moon Bay Marina and more recently the Lions Clubs of New Zealand, who since 1999 have responded generously to an annual national appeal, raising over $66,000 to sponsor annual voyages on *Spirit of New Zealand*.

My son Bevan, who was on [disabled Voyage 315A, May 2000] had the most wonderful time. He keeps in touch with half a dozen other children he formed friendships with while on board. I cannot tell you how much enjoyment he got from the trip, not only meeting many wonderful people, but he came home with a whole new perspective.

My husband and I hadn't realised how much [not being able to get his driver's licence] was affecting him until he returned from the voyage, a completely different person. I haven't seen him so happy in a long time and I truly thank you and all the wonderful staff and crew for everything you did.

You provided the opportunity for Bevan to see that life is a gift, and there are many people out there with disabilities, and you just have to make the most out of life, being thankful for what you have, not worrying about what you don't have.

Thank you again from the bottom of our hearts for everything you did.

(Abridged)

MICHELLE McCARTHY
Parent of trainee

OUR VOLUNTEERS

BARRY THOMPSON

VOLUNTEERS HAVE LONG been seen as important to adventure sail-training organisations. Like many sail-training ships, *Spirit of Adventure* carried volunteer watch officers from the start, to complement her professional crews. However, what is unusual in our case has been the Trust Board's willingness to hand over the ship to volunteer masters and mates.

This all began one day in 1975 when Ken Aldridge, a fellow Auckland Coastguard lecturer, suggested that we might give Coastguard boating students some practical teaching afloat. 'How about using *Spirit of Adventure* during the weekends when she returns to Auckland at the end of each ten-day youth voyage?' he asked.

The four original volunteer masters: Captains Con Thode, Jim Varney, Mel Bowen and Barry Thompson.

There was a problem of course. The permanent crew needed their weekend break and we could not expect to generate enough income to pay for an additional crew. The answer was to enlist a volunteer crew and we soon had four keen volunteer masters, Captains Mel Bowen, Jim Varney, Con Thode and Barry Thompson. More masters followed later (see Appendix 4 for a complete list). Other mariners, now shore-based, like Ron Blackman, and stalwarts like Ivor Sanders, soon joined as first and second mates, while Don Burfoot, Stuart Birnie and some of their colleagues became our first volunteer engineers.

But what about cooks? That was a more difficult problem. Someone suggested, 'Why not try the cookery school at the Auckland Technical Institute?' When I spoke to Ted Bryant, the school's supervisor, and suggested his students might be interested, he quickly replied, 'The students be damned. The staff would be keen!' And so we had our cooks!

With marine certificates aplenty, we had no difficulty staffing *Spirit of Adventure* well in excess of the Ministry of Transport's requirements. All we now had to do was to convince the Trust Board that these adult weekend voyages would benefit the Trust, raising its profile among adults and making money too. There was some scepticism at first, but the Board agreed and the first adult weekend voyage took place in March 1976.

After two successful weekend voyages teaching Coastguard members, we extended the scheme to the Auckland night schools that ran boating classes. Tutors joined their students on board for a weekend. From there the whole idea gathered momentum. Although the original weekend voyages were essentially for navigation training, before long we were offering the ship to almost any groups that might like to charter her and learn a little about sailing and safe boating. She was popular with Rotary and Lions clubs, yacht clubs and all sorts of other associations.

Later we offered her to the wider public. There were few more enthusiastically supported weekend voyages than those exclusively for women, who saw them as an opportunity to enjoy a weekend of sailing and 'liberation' from families and the kitchen sink. The tales of weekends afloat were soon widely recounted and they became 'the thing to do'. All who sailed on them enjoyed the experience, guests and volunteers alike.

Following a meeting in November 1984, this group of weekend volunteers grew into the more formal Volunteer Crew Association, known to us all as the VCA. A wonderful spirit of camaraderie soon built among the volunteer crew, and many a good yarn was spun as we met together in the great cabin after a hard day's sailing. Oh, how the old cabin lamp was swinging again!

At one time the volunteers from all over New Zealand keen to crew our two ships numbered several hundred, and several volunteers later became permanent crew. The names of some of our mates, engineers and cooks, from all over the country and far too many to single out for special mention, have become almost legendary. Each brought his or her special skills and personality to assist us. Without them the ships would simply have remained fast alongside the wharf, as the Trust could not have afforded to operate weekend voyages without volunteers.

In short, the weekend voyages out of Auckland and later, the southern ports, were a great success. However, by the mid-1990s, with more demands on most people's leisure time, numbers of both volunteers and adult participants for weekend voyages were declining.

Slowly the scheme wound down, but for about twenty years these voyages were a valuable addition to the Trust's main activity, the ten-day youth voyages. Enjoying sailing in the ship, many adults gained a better understanding of the work the Trust was doing for youngsters and they offered their support in various ways. Many donated their time and skills most generously, while the income from the voyages was a valuable addition to the Trust's finances.

THE WATCH OFFICER'S LAMENT

To the tune of 'One More Star in the Sky' from Joseph and his Amazing Technicolour Dreamcoat.

One more trainee is seasick,
Nineteen are over the side,
Five are convinced they are dying,
And two are sure they have died.

A new one's gone on the wheel,
He stares at the compass pop-eyed,
He's thirty degrees off his set course,
Oh gawd! We've just gone and gybed.

The anchor is jammed in its housing,
The radar's gone on the blink,
The tin tank is stuck in its davits,
The rubber duck is starting to sink.

The bowsprit luff is all baggy,
The 'man overboard' is asleep,
The night watch has footfalls like thunder,
I don't think they *know* how to creep.

The teak is splattered with sun cream,
The sheets are slippery with oil,
Bikinis are busting all over,
The third mate's blood's on the boil.

The lazarette's full of wet sneakers,
The rigging's covered with towels,
The dryer is full of wet knickers,
The foul weather gear is just *foul*.

The galley reeks of wet tea towels,
The saloon of brasso and vim,
The mess deck's awash with deod'rant —
The great cabin's taken to gin.

TESSA DUDER
Written for the Tenth Anniversary Ball, 1983.

MANAGING CHANGE IN DIFFICULT TIMES

BILL MCCOOK

*Bill McCook, operations director and CEO for the Spirit of Adventure Trust
for eight years, came from an engineering and business background, with
extensive sailing and racing experience in the Pacific and around the New Zealand
coast and Hauraki Gulf. He managed the Trust's rapid expansion through times
of great economic, social and educational change.*

We came,
Different,
Vast.
Now we end,
Different,
Close.
We knew
Nothing of each other,
Our lives, hopes, dreams.
Now we share these,
We understand these,
And we cherish these.
We will leave soon
Will we be sad?
Or happy for our time.
Will we write?
Or are memories enough
Reassured am I
That the Spirit of
Our friendship
Our adventure
Will remain
Different,
Close,
Secure.

CARLY WILLIAMSON
Trainee, Voyage 447
(*Spirit of Adventure*, 1994)

I JOINED the Spirit of Adventure Trust at the end of 1986 and left in April 1995. This was a period of great development and change in the history of the Trust, reflected by the three titles that I held over the eight years that I was 'at the helm'.

Starting as the operations director just a few months after *Spirit of New Zealand* was commissioned, I found myself at a critical point in the Trust's history, as it changed from an organisation running a small sail-training vessel to one that was now operating a small shipping company with two ships and a paid staff of around fifteen sea-going and seven shore staff.

The Trust had become a sizeable adventure business, with educational and youth development programmes, hospitality and accommodation requirements, while supporting a large national club of volunteers, supporters and Voyagers who assisted in operations. Though headed by professionals, the volunteers were expected to perform as professional crew members, 'as if employed'.

The maritime industry and regulatory authority were also changing at this time to an auditable, self-managed form of safety management and control for all aspects of shipping in New Zealand, in line with international practices. For the Trust, this meant a radical change from an annual survey inspection and certification, which one year, arbitrarily and without prior warning, insisted on the replacement of all *Spirit of Adventure*'s rigging. This was without regard to many factors, including a proper technical assessment or any consideration for the actual requirements of a 'sailing ship'; both *Spirit*s were then considered to be fully crewed commercial 'cargo vessels'.

Soon after, the regulatory authority began the transformation to the safe ship management model, requiring owners to be responsible, in the Trust's case, for operating sailing ships at all times in a safe and proper manner.

Three major factors compounded our problems. There was the totally unexpected marine inspectors' requirement to replace all *Spirit of Adventure*'s rigging, at a cost to the Trust of around $50,000. The 1987 stockmarket crash, world recession and the burden of very high interest rates — over 20 percent at one stage — further compounded the third problem, the 'start-up' debits incurred with

Spirit of New Zealand's commissioning. She was in effect neither fully paid for nor fully completed when she was launched in February 1986, and her first annual survey and 'completion costs', along with her initial debit, were brought into the day-to-day operations as large and unexpected cost burdens of around $200,000.

My role as the Trust's operations director, with responsibility for all the day-to-day operations, fundraising and overall financial management, was frequently a difficult one over the years. Volunteers, not able to be given and therefore to appreciate the whole financial picture, were often unable to understand the need for financial restraint, or our need to raise significant funds each year just to remain financially in the same place. Potential benefactors perceived us as a successful organisation with no needs, or were under the illusion that it was the 'Fisher family' who provided the required funds. Fundraising for new capital expenditure, such as *Spirit of Adventure*'s rebuild, was always reasonably easy, while raising funds to cover 'historical' expenditure, such as *Spirit of New Zealand*'s construction cost overruns, was almost impossible.

There were, however, opportunities for some creative thinking. We instigated the leadership and management courses for older trainees, where full costs paid by participants meant a small profit could be made.

Then one weekend in 1987 *Spirit of New Zealand* had a free weekend, so I contacted some Auckland City police friends and asked them 'if they had some kids who could use a weekend away'.

The young people who arrived on the wharf I recognised as being like myself many years before, without the opportunities to step out in the world in a positive and socially acceptable fashion. My own childhood was the significant factor in the twenty years that I've been involved with youth work. I was a product of the Second World War, never knew my father and grew up on the 'wrong side of

Trainees swimming off *Spirit of New Zealand*, Great Barrier Island, 1997.

the tracks'. At school I had one teacher who took a particular interest in my abilities whereas many of the others felt that I was the kid 'least likely to succeed'. This teacher saw not my scholastic skills but my apparent ability to be upfront, progressive and to think 'outside the square'.

It was with this background influencing my personal interest, and in collaboration with senior probation and police officers, judges and others, that the ARK (At Risk Kids) Trust was born. Activities were based on a six-month programme of events, including weekends on both *Spirit* ships, and were specifically designed to develop self-esteem and other positive aspects in young people who were failing to meet the requirements of society. The ARK Trust ran for some twelve years, complementing the work that the Spirit Trust was doing, and refocused about 300 young people, some from quite neglected backgrounds.

Some years earlier the Trust Board had made a commitment to attend the 1988 Australian Bicentennial celebrations. This huge operation was planned, fundraised for and executed in four stages: Auckland to Melbourne, Hobart, Sydney and return to Auckland, and with *Spirit of Adventure*'s 1997 visit to the Kermadecs, constitute the only off-shore ventures by the Trust.

By early 1990, the day-to-day management requirements of the Trust could no longer be managed through the complex, time-consuming and cumbersome committee structure, whereby Trust Board members headed a designated sub-committee and reported back. The committee system was scrapped and my role was changed to executive director.

The 1990 New Zealand Sesquicentennial celebrations began with a tall ships event in Gisborne, moving to the Bay of Islands and concluding with a parade of sail up Auckland's Waitemata Harbour. The opening ceremony for the Commonwealth Games had the ships all anchored in line across the harbour to mark the passage of the Queen's baton and comprised the biggest fleet of sailing ships assembled in New Zealand for many years. The sail-

A RAID

It was an all-girls' trip on *Spirit of Adventure*. We were working our way back towards Auckland. *Spirit of New Zealand* had not long sailed from Auckland and we learned she was in the Motuihe Island area of the Hauraki Gulf. Someone suggested a raid. The girls were all for it and hatched a plan.

We made a short night sail to get close to *Spirit of New Zealand* but remained out of sight. With suitable safety protocols in place, one of the mates and several of the girls snuck off in the 'tin tank', our aluminium dinghy. They got aboard *Spirit of New Zealand* in the time-honoured fashion of going up the anchor cable, bypassed a vigilant night watch and entered the cabins. A few eggs were placed on cabin floors, a couple taped to the clapper of the ship's bell and the flag halyard hidden. A suitable message was left on the whiteboard in the after cabin. The raiders returned by the same route and got back aboard *Spirit of Adventure* without being detected. We then anchored near *Spirit of New Zealand* for the night.

The following morning there was the odd bit of disgruntled communication from the other ship. They were not pleased. At about five minutes before 8am we mustered on the after deck for colours and those aboard *Spirit of New Zealand* did the same. We rang eight bells a bit early, and then watched the other ship. We could not hear what was being said but there was a fair bit of animation between the mate John Reeve ('JR') and the poor trainee sent to bend the ensign on. The realisation that the flag halyard was missing sent JR into a spin. I don't think I've seen him move so fast looking for a substitute halyard, piece of string, or anything at all to raise the flag. More disgruntled communication.

For the record, I have to make the point that girls are far more cunning and devious in these undertakings than boys!
MIKE FOSTER

ing ships *Young Endeavour, Tradewind, R Tucker Thompson, Søren Larsen, Breeze, Spirit of Adventure* and *Spirit of New Zealand* all took part. I was proud to take a leadership role in organising this event, and later to receive a 1990 Commemorative Queen's Service Medal.

During this time the Trust also supported a number of overseas sail-training organisations to start up or develop their operations, in line with what had become the Spirit of Adventure Trust's internationally recognised youth development methods and programmes.

The most notable of these were the Australian youth development ships *Alma Doepel, Leeuwin* and *Young Endeavour* and the Japanese sail training ship *Akogare* established by the Port of Osaka. The Trust Board's representatives, management and sea-going staff spent time in both Australia and Osaka, with the ships' crews coming to New Zealand to sail with us, learning how we managed a large and complex organisation accommodating thousands of people a year.

We also began formal working relationships with other New Zealand adventure programmes, when Outward Bound, the Outdoor Pursuits Centre and the Spirit of Adventure Trust started meeting regularly together to develop professional adventure standards.

In addition to these external activities and the ongoing financial issues, there came the requirement for management responsibility, for 'safe ship management systems', requiring operational manuals, documentary procedures and other formal and audited evidence that the 'shipping business' was operating safely. Many of the colour-coded manuals on how all the aspects of the Trust's two ships operated were produced at this time to meet the new maritime operational rules. A crisis management plan had also been developed and was successfully used by the incoming CEO John Lister, when *Spirit of New Zealand* ran aground at Great Barrier Island in September 1995. My role was pivotal to these requirements, and in 1991 my title changed again, to that of the Trust's chief executive officer.

I left the Trust in April 1995, with two ships in pristine condition. *Spirit of Adventure* had just completed an almost total rebuild and the Trust's financial position was significantly improved from where it was eight years before. I believe, with the help of my great staff, principally Pippa Tizzard, and the committed volunteers the Spirit of Adventure Trust attracts, I left an organisation which had risen to the challenges of those years of great change and was more able to manage itself professionally into the future.

My heart lies in youth and their related development and educational issues. Today I am still involved in roles that work to fix a school system which often, I believe, fails many young people who have talents outside academia.

Captain Nick Hylton with Maori warriors during the 1990 sesquicentennial celebrations in which the Spirit of Adventure Trust took part.
(Dominion Post)

LOOKING BACK

J IM V ARNEY

Former Auckland harbourmaster Jim Varney was one of the Spirit of Adventure Trust's original four volunteer masters. He became a member of the Trust Board in 1980 and deputy chairman in 1998. Jim retired from the Trust Board in 2002.

Early in May 1976 I received a call from Captain Stan Hulford, operations manager for the Trust at that time. He asked me if I could take ten days off to sail as a volunteer second mate on *Spirit of Adventure*. I'd never spoken to Stan before and knew very little about the ship or her operation. This didn't worry him as they needed the certificate and in a hurry, so in sailors' parlance I did a 'pier-head jump', my first but not the last as far as *Spirit* was concerned.

Little did I realise that it was to lead to 26 years of active participation with the 'Spirit family'. I, like so many other people from all walks of life who have completed a voyage on a *Spirit*, had become hooked for life.

An estimated 3500 people walked through the ship as she lay in the Whangarei Town Basin looking spic and span after a frantic rush to clean and air her once we reached the calm waters off Marsden Point. We'd been blown off our anchorage on the outer fringe of Mansion House Bay, Kawau, in the early hours of the morning and had to motor into a northerly gale and a very nasty sea up the coast, with the lee side full of youngsters competing to win the chunderthon.

Those of you who've had the pleasure of attempting to sleep, or indeed working below, in such conditions would be well aware of the state of the accommodation on arrival at the Heads. The girls did a magnificent job and as we came alongside all hands were neatly attired and 'fallen in' in their watches. I could hardly credit the transformation in attitude of these young women, and this was only halfway through the trip. The sense of pride they exhibited in 'their ship' was apparent to all,

a factor I was to encounter many times over the years on port visits or when chatting to Voyagers years after their trip.

Later that year the adult weekends were introduced, crewed in most cases entirely by volunteers, with Barry Thompson, Mel Bowen, Con Thode and myself as the original masters. The weekends proved not only an excellent source of income for the Trust, but great public relations, with some organisations making them an annual event.

In Wellington one weekend in February 1980, at the end of a day sail for handicapped teenagers (plus a few VIPs), Stephen Fisher came down to the aft cabin for a quiet chat, concluding with an invitation to join the Trust Board. I accepted, and regard it as one of my better spur-of-the-moment decisions.

In April, together with Penny Whiting and Fred Huddleston, I was duly inducted on to the Board and perhaps for the first time realised the legacy that Lou Fisher had bequeathed to the nation and the mammoth task that his son and the Board faced in achieving the stated aim: 'To offer equal opportunity to young New Zealanders to develop qualities of leadership, independence and community spirit through the medium of the sea.'

There can be no doubt that under Stephen Fisher's able chairmanship this aim has been, and is being, fulfilled. I am equally certain that all Board members past and present would acknowledge that without the support, goodwill and dedication of both voluntary and paid staff members of the Spirit family, this would not have been possible.

INTO THE NEW MILLENNIUM

The new millennium dawns behind CEO John Lister on board *Spirit of New Zealand*, Gisborne, 1 January 2000.

John Lister

John Lister came to the Spirit of Adventure Trust as CEO in 1995 with wide business and fundraising experience in the corporate sector and for sporting and charitable organisations. He was awarded an OBE in 1986 for his services to exports.

IN 1995, after only six employment positions in a working life of forty years, each involved in the people business and each one an enjoyable experience, I became CEO of the Spirit of Adventure Trust.

I was rather conned into the position by Stephen Fisher, chair of the Trust Board, which was at the time looking for a new CEO. He asked me to advise the Board on the qualities, qualifications and experiences a CEO should have. I did that, but didn't recognise that his flattery was sucking me into the position until finally he smiled and said, 'Why don't you do the job?' Eight years on, I'm pleased my current position has proved so enjoyable and continually challenging.

I could never have imagined my sporting life starting with a P-class and my working life finishing with *Spirit of New Zealand*, that beautiful, traditional square-rigger now regarded as a New Zealand icon.

These days, managers don't always have a passion for or knowledge of the product or service they are managing. My father told me salesmen are born, and he was one of the best. From age ten, when I was serving in our family shop, I realised that I could motivate others by showing or explaining benefits to them. Today's business culture, even for charities like ours, is tough; you must make decisions from your head, not from your heart.

At the beginning of my time with the Trust, not many of the Spirit team perceived me as anything other than a successful businessman, marketer and fundraiser, certainly not especially a sea lover at heart, born and raised beside a beach, Scorching Bay in Wellington. I sailed my first boat at seven, a P-class at ten, Idlealongs and then 14-foot 'X'ies, representing Wellington in the Sanders Cup for three years with some success. Having moved to Auckland, I sailed with the Royal New Zealand Yacht Squadron on K-class yachts and then Stewart 34s.

When I joined the Spirit, the Trust Board set me three objectives:
- To return the Trust to profitability after a difficult period following the 1987 crash, the era of Ruthernomics and changes like Tomorrow's Schools;
- To run the business at a breakeven or better;
- To establish our own operations office accommodation.

I had every reason to believe that with the culture of teamwork already established by the Trust Board, the staff and the many volunteers involved, these objectives would only take time, energy and persistence. (Indeed, the third was to take seven years.)

However, within four months of joining, I was on my way south with my family for a well-earned skiing holiday. We got off the plane in Queenstown, feeling no pain after three stops at the Koru lounge on the way down. From habit, I turned on the cellphone. 'You have ten messages, press one,' and so on.

It was Paul Leppington's voice, the last I wanted to hear. '*Spirit of New Zealand* is ashore on Great Barrier, Tryphena Harbour. All trainees off safely. Best you get back right away.'

And yes, I swore before my next thought, which was, what the hell do I do now? Is there a crisis management plan? Has it been tried? Where is it?! Yes, there was, and it was in my briefcase.

I soon discovered that the Auckland team was already in full action mode, with Captain Leppington and his crew brought in by chopper to set up the salvage team at Great Barrier Island. The operations office staff were already back at the office (it was, sod's law, a Saturday), working with trainees' transport homewards and responding to anxious parents who had picked up the news bulletins on radio. Volunteers literally in their dozens were offering their help, all of which needed to be managed.

By the time I was nearing Auckland Airport, the Board's maritime advisers, Captains Barry Thompson and Jim Varney, had already set up Salvage HQ in my offices, leaving me the media coordination. And yes, reporters were at Auckland Airport to meet me, wanting a statement. All they got was, 'No comment now, I need to talk to my team.'

As expected, there were front page stories the next day in all the New Zealand papers, with photographs of our beautiful ship lying on her side, high and dry, and very undignified. The story led that night's television news, and there was huge media interest worldwide: CNN News, Channels 7 and 10 in Australia, all positive and sympathetic until some local fisherman, who'd mounted an ill-judged and futile rescue attempt during the night in his boat, saw an opportunity to slag off an organisation that supposedly catered for Auckland rich kids.

That grounding and its often uncomfortably public aftermath was to preoccupy me for the next twelve months and delay the fundraising programme I wanted to develop, but the way we managed it was testament to the culture of teamwork which, as we taught our trainees, was the key to successful relationships and living. Great teamwork had ensured that the trainees were all off the ship safely and on the way home, and the ship herself was refloated five days later with no major damage.

History has now shown that we were very lucky in the recovery of the vessel. The southerly storm that put her ashore had quickly abated and there were still five more extreme high tides that would assist her refloating. A Navy dive team was quickly on hand and available to research the best position on the sandy beach to refloat her; amazingly six tugs were also close by, providing over 100,000 tonnes of pulling power. It really seemed like all New Zealand was there to help us.

When the ship went aground she actually crossed two sandbanks; there were many so-called experts advising us on the best way to refloat. Some of the locals were very critical of our decisions, but they had less knowledge than the Navy dive team that spent considerable time blasting sand away from her keel and exploring the channels that led towards deeper water. After three days and nights of sandblasting and six tugs pulling, we were able to move *Spirit* across the innermost sandbank and parallel along the beach to a deeper channel.

After each high tide and the effort made by our teams, *Spirit* would gracefully lie on her side like a stranded whale waiting to go back to sea. Then an amazing phenomenon happened. On the last high tide of day four *Spirit* chose to sit perfectly upright looking out to sea and we could tell that she was ready to be refloated. Sure enough, on the last of the high tides, day five, I received the call from Paul that we had all been waiting for: 'We're afloat and on our way to Tauranga.' It was an enormous relief for all and amazing how New Zealand rejoiced. This time it was a good news story for all the media.

Two days later *Spirit* was dry-docked at Tauranga. We were all surprised and relieved how little damage she had sustained. In fact, the soft sand of Tryphena Harbour had done no damage, the sandblasting had cleaned her hull satisfactorily and inspection showed no structural concerns at all. After receiving the MSA recer-

I had the pleasure of being on Voyage 201 of the Spirit *that ran aground on Great Barrier Island. It was an amazing experience for all and we enjoyed it thoroughly. Thanks for a great first trip. Could you please let me know as soon as possible when my next trip is so I can plan Christmas holiday employment.* (Abridged)
MATTHEW PERKINS
Trainee, Voyage 201, 1995

I was on Voyage 201, in August. Although it was a tragedy that the ship became stuck in soft sand, and our expedition was cut short, I look forward to returning. At no time was I scared or anxious at the thought of having to evacuate our ship. Because of this I would like to thank the crew, and especially our Captain Paul Leppington for their thoughtfulness. I am glad that this crew guided us through the days we sailed upon Spirit of New Zealand. *Thank you for the experiences I achieved, and I look forward to my return.*
BELINDA ALLEN
Trainee, Voyage 201, 1995

tification, *Spirit of New Zealand* was refloated at Tauranga, took 40 new trainees aboard, and headed off back to sea.

We lost only one ten-day voyage and all those forty lucky trainees were repositioned in voyages over the next few months to resume their lifetime experience.

As expected, there was a full marine enquiry with the ship's master being charged under the Marine Act. Surprisingly, he pleaded not guilty, but after four days of cross-examination he changed his plea to guilty. He was convicted, fined and censured.

This was almost the end of the saga, except for the battle that remained with the insurers as to what was and wasn't covered. The debates that followed made me a far better educated CEO on insurance matters. It was no great surprise when the Trust Board changed its underwriters the following year, to a worldwide owners' insurance club.

The 1995 grounding could have become a shipwreck which would have destroyed the ongoing integrity and history of the Trust. It was the teamwork of the marine advisers, crew, volunteers and others which together contributed to a successful recovery and resumption of routine activities.

Two years later the Trust Board grappled with the difficult but inevitable decision to sell *Spirit of Adventure*. The financial and administrative burden of running two ships was inescapable. She was 25 years old and becoming uneconomic to operate as a youth development ship. On Sunday 17 August, at a moving wharf-side ceremony attended by our Patron, the then governor-general Sir Michael Hardie Boys, and 200 invited guests, the white ship was officially decommissioned. We made some new friends, particularly her new owners Captain Cook Cruises in Fiji, and lost a few, some loyal but saddened volunteers who couldn't agree with the commercial decision to sell her.

The America's Cup regattas between 1995 and 2003 also demonstrated the

FOOD FOR THOUGHT...

Imagine you're on the *Spirit*, lying out on the bowsprit
Hear the sound of the water against the hull
Feel the breeze against your face
Listen to ropes creaking, to people talking, to people laughing
Feel the heat from the sun
Look up and see people on the yards
Close your eyes
Breathe

Smile

Poem by trainee, Voyage 348, July 2001
(Andy Belcher)

Spirit team at its very best. The Trust chose to be involved in the two Team New Zealand defences of the Cup. This decision, at minimal cost to the ten-day youth voyage programme, proved to be not only a worthwhile financial success, but also a stunning public relations exercise involving many of our people and greatly increasing the awareness of what we achieve on our ten-day trips on board *Spirit of New Zealand*.

Being wing mark in the first defence and windward mark in the second promoted the vessel to a worldwide audience and certainly assisted us in marketing *Spirit* as a spectator ship to many of the Trust's friends. Excited guests, the maximum number allowed, were accommodated on board for every race for both the Louis Vuitton and the America's Cups. With the ship sporting specially fitted wide-screen television and bars, they were well catered for by professional and dedicated volunteer crews who all helped to make their days memorable in every respect.

The Trust benefited by over half a million dollars from these two charter opportunities, but that is only half the story. The involvement of volunteers nationwide in something other than our normal activity brought out the very best in them all. The increased knowledge and awareness also resulted in greater interest within the schools by trainees, and by others wishing to utilise the vessel when not involved in youth development programmes.

Let's also reflect on the late Sir Peter Blake, a wonderful friend of the Trust. Through his leadership of Team New Zealand 2000, and that organisation's obligation as a registered charity to put money back into the community, a donation of $500,000 was made to the Trust to assist us with our half-life refit and build up the Team New Zealand Spirit Scholarship fund which offers fee subsidies to deserving trainees.

Moving the administration offices six times in as many years has been another saga, and the toughest of my three objectives to achieve on a sustainable, long-term basis. From Marsden Wharf we moved to new, spacious and apparently permanent offices on Prince's Wharf, only to find them bulldozed to the ground as the new Prince's Wharf development got under way two years later. Then came four years in the infamous, cramped and in summer impossibly hot portacoms by the entrance to Prince's Wharf. During the millennium summer, with construction continuing on the Prince's Wharf complex and milling Cup crowds right outside their windows, my staff knew that once their small offices hit 30° C, they were free to stop work and go home. From the portacoms we moved twice, from the 12th to the 16th floor of the HSBC Building at No. 1 Queen Street. Negotiations for the resource consent for our new permanent home on the eastern end of the National Maritime Museum building went on — and on — for nearly three years, but reached a happy conclusion at the end of 2002, with the new office building completed and occupied in August 2003.

The opening of our new permanent offices adjacent to the Maritime Museum's facility is a fitting celebration to mark the Trust's 30th birthday. At last our offices are alongside our berth close by the Viaduct Basin in the Auckland central business district. After successfully running both a national maritime and educational organisation for 30 years, I believe the Trust has earned the right to be there, and the yards of its fine ship to grace the historic Hobson Basin.

I've now completed to my satisfaction the three objectives set back in 1995, but many have helped me achieve these: a dedicated and professional Board who backed everything that I wanted or recommended; loyal staff who must have often wondered where I was going and how I was going to achieve it; the many supporters of the Trust who have proved their loyalty, such as the Ports of Auckland, the Kitchener Group, ASB and Waikato Charitable Trusts, City of Auckland leaders and the officers of the Auckland City Council and Auckland Regional Council. I'm looking forward to further developing a long-term and harmonious relationship with our near neighbours, the National Maritime Museum of New Zealand Trust Board and its staff.

This is a people organisation. Strong leadership is important, but it only works if you're all on board and sailing in the same direction. Every one of us in Team Spirit, either paid or unpaid, has adopted the Trust as their chosen charity and gives their time freely. I've felt comfortable in my leadership role, in particular when it has been associated with special projects or event management, such as the America's Cup charters and the new premises.

So, with the America's Cup party over, a sound ship, great crew and the shore staff sitting in brand-new permanent offices, what's ahead for the Trust?

There's the unglamorous but constant challenge of simply sustaining the high standards we set ourselves. Continuing to develop our worldwide recognised youth development programme. The enormous effort required to raise $10,000 each and every week, crucial if the Trust wishes to maintain the trainee fee subsidy of about 40 percent of the real voyage cost. It's a target I personally believe in.

The Trust may need to address the decline of the regional support structure, now 20-odd years old. We're not getting the new volunteers or the Voyagers coming through to serve on committees as we did in the good old days of ten or fifteen years ago. Regional Associations are now being run and supported by many who have done long service for the Trust, and in Spirit terms that can mean over ten or even twenty years.

We're a national organisation and long may that remain, but with today's communications and systems, management could and should be centralised. That begs the question: 'Should we take the ship to the trainees, or the trainees to the ship?'

The Trust must soon turn its attention to the replacement of *Spirit of New Zealand*. Thankfully the Foundation's investments in forestry and other interests will go a long way towards funding a new ship in approximately ten to twelve years. We'll need at least $20,000,000, a major fundraising task.

THE AMERICA'S CUP

WHEN NEW ZEALAND won the America's Cup in 1995, the Spirit of Adventure Trust chose to become involved in the four subsequent regattas: two Louis Vuitton Challenger Series and two America's Cup defences. Through the Trust's association with the Royal New Zealand Yacht Squadron and others closely involved in running the regattas, *Spirit of New Zealand* was chosen to be a course mark, one of only two boats located inside the 'course box' for the racing.

In this position, *Spirit of New Zealand* was seen by many on and off the water and received extensive and almost daily television coverage, both locally and internationally. As a spectator vessel her position was unsurpassed and provided ringside seats for an ambitious hospitality programme. Over the four regattas, *Spirit of New Zealand* hosted thousands of guests on board, providing a variety of high quality hospitality programmes, all served with the special 'Spirit' touch.

The office staff and sea crews worked tirelessly at these times. They were joined by teams of volunteers who came from all over New Zealand, at their own expense, to work on board the ship and behind the scenes during the four regattas. Much of their work was less than glamorous. Cleaning the heads and emptying the rubbish bins was as much a part of the role for many as attending to the guests on deck. However, the end result was a very warm, very professional hospitality programme that raised a considerable amount of money for the Trust's coffers. Importantly, the Trust was able to take advantage of this wonderful opportunity to raise funds without compromising many of its ten-day youth development voyages.

The America's Cup benefited the Trust financially in a second important way. Through the leadership of the late Sir Peter Blake, a wonderful friend of the Trust, Team New Zealand 2000 made a very generous donation of $500,000 to the Trust when it was wound up in 2002.

However, the financial benefits are only half the story. The Trust's participation in the regattas went a long way to continuing to develop national awareness of both the ship and the Trust's work with New Zealand's youth. Over the last three years, interest in trainees' berths and the Trust's waiting lists have increased dramatically. Companies and other groups are keen to hire the vessel when she is available, and there has been a significant increase in organisations wishing to fund trainees on ten-day youth development voyages.

Sir Peter Blake at the helm of *Spirit of New Zealand* **on the Waitemata Harbour during the America's Cup 2000.**

A TEACHER'S VIEW

CHRIS BASHAM

Chris Basham was, until recently, a teacher and 'Spirit coordinator' at Avondale College in Auckland. She previously held this role at Whangarei Boys High School.

I HAVE BEEN associated with student voyages on *Spirit of New Zealand* for five years, as the school administrator at Whangarei Boys High School from 1998 to 2000 and at Avondale College since 2001. I have also had the pleasure of sailing on two separate half-day voyages so I know this is a great experience for our students.

Each year the Portage Licensing Trust in West Auckland provides Avondale College with thirteen sponsored berths valued at $900 each. This is wonderful from my point of view as I can select students who would not normally be able to afford this life-changing experience. It also means I have no difficulty in filling the allocated berths. It was much more difficult at my former school, as parents and trainees had to raise money themselves to cover the voyage fees.

We select students through several sources. First, we advertise in the daily notices and students can write a letter stating why they should go. All senior students are considered from this pool. Secondly, I email all staff members —

COMMUNITY SUPPORT: THE PORTAGE LICENSING TRUST

Over the past 30 years community licensing trusts such as the Portage Licensing Trust in West Auckland and service clubs such as Lions and Rotary have provided considerable financial assistance to help young New Zealanders afford a ten-day voyage with the Spirit of Adventure Trust. Their continued support is a clear sign that they believe that young people benefit from a voyage on *Spirit*.

The Portage Trust in West Auckland has been associated with the Spirit of Adventure Trust for three years. Each year, it has funded 40 students from the five secondary schools in its catchment area (Avondale College, Kelston Boys High School, Kelston Girls High School, Green Bay High School and Lynfield College), paying the $900 student contribution to voyage costs in each case. The Portage Trust and the local secondary schools work in partnership, with the Portage Trust providing the funding and the school's Spirit coordinator selecting the students to receive the grant. The selection criteria are the same in all cases: the Trust funds students who would most benefit from a voyage and for whom the costs would otherwise be prohibitive.

'We are overwhelmed by the letters that we receive back from the youngsters we fund,' says the chairman of the Portage Trust, Ross Clow. 'It's very obvious to us that a ten-day voyage on *Spirit of New Zealand* can make a big difference in a young person's life. The schools we deal with often give us examples of young students who go on board shy and lacking confidence and motivation at school and who return ten days later with a new lease on life — enthusiasm, new friendships and direction for the future.'

Morning swim!

Nga mihi nui ki a koe
Tena koe e te rangatira

This year our school has been fortunate to have received sponsorship of $1,500, which has enabled three of our students, two boys and one girl, to undertake voyages on Spirit of Adventure *and* Spirit of New Zealand.

On behalf of the students at the school and the Board of Trustees, I would like to express my genuine appreciation for the support you have given these students. Without such assistance, we would not be able to offer this opportunity to the young people attending our school.

Our school serves a low socio-economic area where there is a lot of goodwill and enthusiasm for educational issues, but unfortunately at this time money is scarce.

Would you please pass on to members of your Trust our very real thanks for the support you have given our young people.
Noho mai ra
Naku noa
Na
A J CRANSHAW
Principal/Tumuaki
Ngaruawahia High School
August 1994

guidance counsellors, deans and form teachers — and ask for nominations for students who in their opinion would most benefit from the experience.

I also visit classes, particularly in the lower streamed bands, to encourage students to step out of their comfort zone and take up the challenge. I then interview all applicants and make a shortlist of fifteen so that I have a backup in the unlikely event that someone pulls out.

The next task is to match allocated berths to students, keeping in mind the correct gender and trying to accommodate sports tournaments, academic commitments including exams, assignments and in-class assessments (Year 13 students try

Being totally blind, I found many interesting challenges on board apart from the handling of the ship. Climbing up the mast in 35-knot winds is not easy, but after coming down I felt a certain exhilaration to know that I had achieved something which many sighted voyagers find difficult.

Overall, the voyage was a lot of fun, and I think everybody learned a lot about disabilities and the different ways they are handled by individuals.
(Abridged)
LISETTE WESSELING
Disabled Trainee
(October 1987)

to take the December berths so their external exams are behind them), drama and dance performances, the talent contest and compulsory class trips.

I also apply for a berth on the disabled voyage each year and have been successful in placing a blind student. This requires a lot of liaison with the student support person at school and the family, and some money needs to be raised for this voyage as it is separate from the thirteen sponsored berths.

Another task is to respond with speed to the Year 10 challenge opportunity offered each year, the Spirit Trophy. This is an inter-school five-day team event and very popular with the students.

Once the students are organised on voyages, the Spirit of Adventure Trust sends out the registration forms in date order. We are lucky to have a full-time nurse at the college who can complete the required medical form with the student. The remaining information is sent home to be signed by parents or caregivers and returned to me at school. There have been rare occasions when the Spirit of Adventure Trust has had to reject a student based on certain medical conditions, but I like to give all students a chance.

When the students return from the trip, they are always full of confidence and brimming over with excitement. I am normally treated to photos, funny stories and many adventures which I keep for our school magazine. The students are expected to write a letter of thanks to the Portage Licensing Trust, which I check and then post on their behalf. At the end of the year the Portage Licensing Trust organises an afternoon tea for all the participants they sponsor from different schools around West Auckland, and students get to share their experiences.

I feel privileged to be involved with the Spirit of Adventure Trust as I have the opportunity to choose students who I believe will really benefit from the experience and then get to see incredible changes made in ten days. Some of the students are shy, lacking confidence and life experience, or are unmotivated at school with no clear future direction.

When I next see them they are focused and positive, have lots of new friends and have a fresh new approach to school and their futures. Students overcome many fears during their voyages — heights, early morning dips jumping into cold, deep sea water, going along the bowsprit, meeting new people, sharing a room with nineteen other strangers and sleeping in a hammock, learning to sail, trying new food and being accepted.

Often the experience is about giving students hope and a new start. Miracles seem to occur on board the ship and this is a credit to the crew, who are obviously very dedicated and skilled at working with youth from all cultures, ages and backgrounds.

Many of the students return to do volunteer work on the ship and some structure their career-planning around outdoor education, the Navy and other marine-based activities as a result of going on *Spirit*. There are also yearly reunions to attend which are popular with students and advertised through our notices at school.

A MAGICAL DAY, JUNE 1992

JANET WATKINS

Janet Watkins joined the Spirit of Adventure Trust as volunteer crew in 1980. Since that time she has crewed in many positions, including mate and watch leader. Janet lives in Auckland, where she is actively involved in youth sailing programmes.

0600 The moon had long since set and all was very dark
The little ship seemed to be floating in space
As sea and land and sky blended in the blackness
And all was silence.
0630 Trainees emerged from the lighted fo'c'sle
And peace was shattered — One! Two! Three! Four...
The splashes, the yells, the early morning dip
That's meant to wake this peaceful, sleepy world.
0700 The calm returned as *Spirit* came to life
A rosy glow warmed the wakening eastern sky.
Still shadowy hills left mirrored images on the silvery
    waters of the bays
And day dawned clear and calm.
We'd been ashore the night before to Smokehouse Cove
And barbecued our sausages on Websters' grill.
We'd sung around the bonfire and paddled back aboard
Across the moonlit bay. (An engine would intrude on
    that still night.)
0815 And in the early sunlight to check that all was tidy
I launched the dinghy and motored for the shore.
The outboard roared defiance to the new day
Bow waves left crumpled grooves upon the glassy sea.
A populous intrusion in a pristine world.

The tide was out, a scallop smiled from three feet down
A flounder left its vapour trail of sand
And so as not to shatter more that calm
I sculled back in silence leaving only little eddies with
    the oar
That gently stirred the oily surface.
0930 We motored out through Governor's Pass and
    south inside the islands.
The rising sun shone from a cloudless sky.

Our perfect mirror image cruised beside
And, as if the water was no longer there,
The fish, the kelp, the rocks as clear as clear
Yet forty feet below.
1230 The sun was at its zenith, not overhead as this
    was June.
All sails were set on *Spirit* as she ghosted.
We took the cameras in the dinghy to photograph
    our ship
As she drifted on a zephyr.
The cloudless sky melted into the flat ocean
New Zealand was hull down and out of sight
A white, white ship suspended in the blue —
Timeless and in a world apart.
We swam and swam beside our phantom ship
And basked on deck in sunshine soft and warm
We had forgotten this was winter time.
1700 The zephyr lifted to a gentle breeze,
We slowly coasted southwards for the night.
This magic day was coming to a close
The sun glowed golden in the western skies.
And as we watched that fireball disappear
It *flashed* that *brilliant green* of myths
    and legends —
The emerald city down the golden road.
It was but a brief moment — and then the night
As on we sailed — with whispering waves and wind.

The incident to which Janet refers at the end of this verse is known as 'the green flash'. This phenomenon is seen only at sunrise and sunset (and then by only a very lucky few!), when part of the sun suddenly changes colour. It is caused by astronomical refraction of colour near the horizon.

A SANITARY TALE

BRUCE MARLER

*During the 1970s Bruce Marler was a founding trustee and volunteer mate
for the Spirit of Adventure Trust, as well as a flag officer for the
Royal New Zealand Yacht Squadron. He and other family members
run a well-known shoe manufacturing business in Auckland.*

IN THE CHRISTMAS-NEW YEAR period immediately following the launch of
Spirit of Adventure in late 1973, my wife Sonia and I had the pleasure of joining
Lou and Iris Fisher and friends for a shakedown cruise in the Bay of Islands. On
issuing the invitation, Lou had explained that, apart from enjoying the company
and the sailing, the main object of the exercise was to 'shake down' the vessel and
prepare her for her busy trainee programme. We were to test the gear and equipment, both above and below decks.

The weather was glorious, the sailing conditions were perfect, and Lou wore a
constant smile — until at breakfast about five days into the cruise when someone
reported that one of the toilets had become blocked. There was an unpleasant
smell emanating from the bilge ...

Fortunately we were at the coffee stage of breakfast by that time and Bill Craike
volunteered to go below and check things out. Fortified by a whisky and milk, followed by two cups of strong coffee, I volunteered to be his assistant. So Pony
More, Bill and I, with the aid of a strong torch, went into the bilge. There in the
torchlight was an unpleasant sight — about four inches of sewage and sea water
sloshing about. We immediately reported back to the saloon where, on Lou's
'motion', supported by Pony, Bill was appointed chief sanitary engineer and I his
assistant.

Lou's quick mind then announced that all hands were to go ashore for a swim
or stroll while we three set about improving the situation. The three of us were
literally 'in it' for about three hours, Bill and I bailing with buckets into a larger
container while Pony attacked the pipes with spanners and drain-unblocking
equipment. Bill's sense of humour prevailed: 'At least it's friendly sewage!'

Just as the shore party was shouting to come aboard and prepare lunch, we were
able to signal the 'all clear!' Now it was our turn to take a swim over the side. We
were absolved from further duties for the rest of the day.

The last night party in the saloon was a hilarious affair with a prizegiving for
winners of various contests throughout the voyage such as navigation, knot tying,
swimming and cooking. Pony presented the last prize of all to Bill Craike. This
was the chief sanitary engineer's award — two beer cans soldered together with
connecting tubing. He tells me he still has it on his mantelpiece in Queensland.

One afternoon, on day one of a ten-day voyage, we were near the eastern end of Tamaki Strait. The time was near for the mandatory 'man overboard' drill. We were more than a little astonished when the captain suddenly jumped over the side. What trust he placed in a group of new trainees and especially in his permanent crew! Obviously our 'about ship' and subsequent pick-up were successful.

BRUCE LETHBRIDGE
Volunteer crew

RISING TO THE CHALLENGE

RONA McCONACHY

Rona McConachy and her husband Peter joined the Trust as volunteer crew in 1986. Since then they have crewed regularly on both ships, Rona in the roles of third and fourth officer and senior watch officer. Rona and Peter were port contacts for Northland from 1987 to 1996. They are retired teachers and since retirement have set up 'Adventure Northland' to raise sponsorship to send needy young people in the region on ten-day youth development voyages. In 1998 they received the Trust Board's coveted Topgallant Award. Rona and Peter live in Whangarei.

WE SAILED OUR YACHT into the calm waters of Whangamumu Harbour and, turning into the wind, dropped anchor. An old whaling station, this land-locked harbour is one of our favourite anchorages on our way up or down the coast between Whangarei and the Bay of Islands. On the stony shore, where a tiny stream flows into the harbour, lie the remains of the whaling station. They consist of several derelict concrete walls, a concrete slipway where the huge whale carcasses were once hauled up for cutting and stripping, and a stone cairn telling the shameful story of the killing of these magnificent creatures.

The different greens of the New Zealand bush stretch up high to the ridges above, while further round the shoreline grass covers a long slope that cradles the head of the harbour. Cliffs encircle the entrance, leaving a narrow gap through which ships once towed the slaughtered whales.

As we always did when anchored safely, we dived over the side into the cold, clear water, marvelling again at the bloody history of this beautiful, tranquil sanctuary. Suddenly we caught sight of two tall masts with white sails moving steadily towards the opening to the harbour. As we watched, a graceful white ship sailed into view, gliding through the water majestically. There was activity everywhere. The jibs were dropping, the mainsail was being stowed along the boom and the anchor made ready for letting go. Slowly the ship came around into the wind. A square sail was lowered. The anchor fell with a loud splash as the ship slowly stopped. The square sail was furled and figures climbed up the ratlines to the yards. The two square sails were expertly tied to the yardarms. It was *Spirit of Adventure*!

'I'm going to call them up,' said Peter. 'I'll ask if we can visit them and look over the ship.'

'*Spirit of Adventure*! *Spirit of Adventure*! This is *Ocelot* ZM 2232

Long-time volunteers and winners of the Topgallant Award, Rona and Peter McConachy.

calling. Are you receiving me?'

'This is *Spirit of Adventure*. Come in *Ocelot*.'

'*Spirit of Adventure*! We are the small yacht to port. Is it possible for us to visit you? Over.'

'*Ocelot*, you are welcome. We will send over the tin tank for you right away. *Spirit of Adventure*! Out.'

A large aluminium dinghy detached itself from the side of the white ship and came noisily over towards us. We climbed down into it, and raced back, avoiding two sailing dinghies manned by trainees and other young people swimming and diving around the ship.

'Climb up the rope ladder,' I was told. It seemed to stretch high, far above my head. Gritting my teeth I grabbed the rope. Up and over the rails I went, finding to my surprise that it was easier than I thought.

A trainee showed us around. We went along the decks to the jibs where the stays disappeared to the top of the mast in a tangle of ropes and wires. We peered into the dark deep locker housing the anchor chain. We looked up at the yardarms. Ropes were everywhere, ropes coming down and ropes going up. There seemed to be hundreds of them.

We followed aft to where the huge boom stretched over to the gleaming wheel and where the main mast had its own vast masses of ropes. Now down the steps we clambered, into the trainees' sleeping quarters, along the companionway where crew members shared tiny cabins, and into the galley where the cook sweated over the gas stove. We were taken up to the mess deck where trainees ate, socialised and listened to lectures, and finally to the officers' mess. Before going down there, I looked over to where *Ocelot*, our yacht, rode at anchor. She looked tidy, trim and familiar!

Paul, the captain, met us. 'Stay and have dinner,' he said. We sat around the large table where there was barely room to move. Trainees brought down dishes of steaming food. Sailing adventures were exchanged.

'You two are just the sort of people we need as volunteer crew on *Spirit of Adventure*,' I heard Paul say. 'You've told me that you have your boatmasters and coastal yachtmasters certificates.'

Abruptly I was jolted out of my enjoyment. My mind leapt to the hundreds of ropes I had seen, and the ratlines leading away up to the yardarms. I remembered the young trainees I had seen working everywhere, and the huge sails.

'Oh no!' I said firmly. 'I've just learned to sail. I don't know enough. Besides that, I would never climb up to the yardarms.'

'You're not meant to know everything,' Paul persuaded. 'You are both teachers and know how to relate to teenagers. That's what's important.'

'I'm interested,' Peter said. 'We've just retired. But both of us must do this together.'

I shook my head emphatically. Captain Paul gave us the forms to fill in.

Later we went down to the Auckland office of the Spirit of Adventure Trust. By chance the beautiful, white schooner was tied up at the wharf. Peter coaxed me to climb just a little way up the ratlines. All of a sudden, I was right up there and out on the yardarms.

It was spellbinding! It was challenging! It was achievement! *Spirit of Adventure* had captured me!

Within a year, I was a watch officer on board that superb sailing ship. But our challenges were only beginning. The voyages on the *Spirit*s became a regular two trips a year, sometimes more. Because we became the port contacts for Northland, there were also adult weekends sailing out from Whangarei.

A trainee secures the gaskets.

What about all those ropes and all those sails? How was it possible to learn 'how, what and where' about them? Before each voyage, the important routine began. The night before Peter and I were due to sail, we sat studying the detailed sketch showing the myriad ropes of *Spirit's* rigging plan. We checked the routines of pulling up sails, then letting them down again. Up went the jibs one by one, the sheets and halyards in the correct places and in the correct order. Then down they came. Once satisfied, more or less, we moved on to the squares, all of them.

In our imagination we climbed out on the yardarms to secure the huge sails with the gaskets after they were furled, remembering how to step carefully on the foot ropes. I groaned when I looked at the diagram with the dozens of ropes attached to the mast.

'I'll never remember all this,' I cried. 'And I'm expected to teach and lead the trainees in my watch!'

Gradually it became easier. With each voyage, my confidence grew. The trainees did not have it all on their own. I too had my challenges as a watch officer. I too discovered strengths I never knew I had.

The superb sailing ship *Spirit of Adventure* has long left New Zealand waters, leaving behind special memories for hundreds of young New Zealanders, of achievements, fellowship, values and shared experiences. Now *Spirit of New Zealand*, the sleek, black barquentine, continues to provide the unique challenges for our youth, in their own voyages of self-discovery.

CRAYFISH FOR BREAKFAST

We were on *Spirit of New Zealand*, lying at anchor a little south of Tairua on the Coromandel Peninsula. A local dive club boat came to visit. The divers came aboard for a short while and we discussed the likely weather conditions for the day. Our parting shot (half joking) was, 'If you get a heap of crayfish, you know where to bring them.'

Later they did return and gave us a lovely crayfish and quite a few scallops. Mate Roger Cooper had a digital camera and took a few photos of this wonderful feast. There were also some shots of mate John Wilson with his face buried into the head of the crayfish and of other crew members thoroughly enjoying themselves. (Of course, I was totally uninvolved in this debauchery!)

Then the scheming began. Overnight, someone sent an email to the Spirit of Adventure operations office outlining the crew's dissatisfaction with the food they were providing us. They attached a montage of these photographs to the email.

At exactly 08:00:30 the following morning Spirit of Adventure Trust CEO John Lister was on the telephone to the ship. Most of what he said is unrepeatable, but the gist was something about his slaving hard in the office while we were on some sort of holiday, gorging ourselves on the fruits of the sea. Apparently the initial message caused quite a stir in the office until the attached photos were opened.

MIKE FOSTER
Master

BECOMING A CREW

GEOFF ROWARTH

Geoff Rowarth became a volunteer master with the Spirit of Adventure Trust in 1984. He continued in this role right up to his death in 1994, sailing on one of the Spirits *just weeks before he died. His son, Neil, is also a volunteer master with the Spirit of Adventure Trust.*

SAIL TRAINING is about living, working and playing with people you haven't met before; about becoming a member of a team. About taking responsibility, giving and taking orders, pushing yourself physically and mentally. Being cold, wet, weary, perhaps sick, often frightened – and looking back on it as the most wonderful experience of your life!

As a crew member of a sail-training ship, you quickly learn that 'they' are no longer there to do things for you: the plumber to fix the tap, Mum to make the bed, the Council to sweep up the litter you drop in the street, the 'takeaways' to provide a quick meal. On board there is only 'us'. If something needs doing, it can only be you, me, him or her, not 'they', who will do it.

Spuds to be peeled, decks to be scrubbed, bunks to be tidied, sails to be set, heads to be unblocked, anchor cable to be stowed. The list is endless, but if nobody does it, it doesn't get done. No spuds peeled, no meal. Cause and effect brought into much closer proximity than usual. If a sail is not adjusted correctly, we cannot point the ship where we want to go, which means it will take an hour longer to reach our destination, which means bed an hour later, which means an hour less sleep. QED, as we used to say in geometry.

Another early lesson is that it is easier if a team works together. One person cannot get the mainsail up; six pulling together do it with ease. But to pull together, someone has to say 'heave' and if someone has had the forethought to rig a block and tackle, we can get it really tight. Slowly the need for discipline and self-discipline is accepted. By the end of a ten-day voyage, what started as a group of 25 disparate individuals, some shy, some nervous, a few suspicious or rebellious, and nearly all totally inexperienced young landlubbers, has become a crew.

They are now 'shipmates' and what they have learned goes far beyond seamanship and navigation.

TEN-DAY VOYAGE ROUTINE

No two voyages are ever the same, as so much depends on factors such as wind direction and strength and the complement of young people on board. However, this is a typical voyage schedule.

DAY 1
Morning: Trainees embark. Ship provisioned. Trainees meet one another and become familiar with the ship.
Afternoon: Ship sails to a local anchorage.
Evening: General discussion.

DAY 2
Morning: Safety lectures.
Afternoon: Training in sail-handling.
Evening: Ship sails to anchorage.

DAY 3 TO DAY 8
Morning and
Afternoon: Point-to-point sailing and adventure training.
Evening: Ship sails to anchorage.

DAY 9
Morning: Trainees elect own master and watch officers and sail ship on pre-set course from A to B.
Afternoon and
Evening: End of voyage function; awards day.

DAY 10
Morning: Ship motors to port of disembarkation. Trainees clean ship en route. Ship secured alongside at 0800. Trainees leave ship.

A TYPICAL DAY ON A TEN-DAY VOYAGE

Again, the schedule for a particular day will depend on a number of factors, including weather.

0600   Call the hands. Exercises on deck. Swim. Clear up mess deck. Duty watch assist cook.
0700   Breakfast followed by clean ship.
0800   Colours. Continue to clean ship.
0900   Instruction and sailing.
1200   Lunch.
1300   Carry on with activities: instruction, sailing, rowing, adventure training.
1900   Dinner (or, if sailing, split into two watches; one watch eats while other watch sails ship).
2030   Evening activity.
2230   Lights out. Two trainees are always on one-hour night watches.

PART 3

SELF-DISCOVERY

TAKING RISKS

GILLIAN BRECKELL

*Gillian Breckell, then a pupil of Macleans College, sailed on Voyage 252
early in 1998. Since then she has finished a business degree, done an
Air Training Corps course and been bungy jumping, skydiving, glacier
climbing, gliding and flying. She currently works in an IT company
while furthering multimedia studies.*

THE 6AM SWIM

One outstanding trainee was a slip of a lass whose home was a very few kilometres from Foveaux Strait. Because of the cold there, she had never swum in sea water. Her immediate challenges were climbing the mast and going over the side for the early morning swim. Once she had literally taken the plunge she blossomed, and one could see her personality developing daily. Ten days later she left the ship a completely different person to the extent that, on the final night, she was awarded a special personal presentation amid acclaim. A fine example of the positive outcome of sail training.

BRUCE LETHBRIDGE
Volunteer crew

Previous page: Voyagers crewing *Spirit of New Zealand* on the Waitemata Harbour during the America's Cup regatta, **March 2003**.

SOME SAY the darkest hour is the hour before the dawn. I say the darkest hour is one when you weigh up the risks and make a decision that will affect your future.

One of my darkest hours was quite literally dark in all aspects. It was around 1 am on a chilly summer morning in 1998 as a group of us stretched, yawned and disembarked from the bus on which we'd travelled from Auckland to Opua in the Bay of Islands. I stood on a wharf and gazed in growing apprehension at the looming bulk of a ship, desperately trying to make myself believe that all those ropes and masts could not possibly belong to one vessel — *Spirit of New Zealand.* That moment, when I stood by the silhouetted shape with its web of rigging spanning the night sky, I faced my first moment of truth.

When I gingerly stepped aboard the ship I understood that I was in a different world. The people crowding around me carrying items aboard stumbled into unfamiliar objects and slipped past obstacles. It was a situation entirely unlike any other I had experienced, and my senses were reeling. Whatever conceptions I had of the world surrounding me were now null and void. This was new, this was different, and I would have to take each day as a separate moment in time. The voyage I was embarking upon was not just a voyage on the sea with 39 other young people like myself, but more the start of a journey of self-realisation, and for some a journey of self-actualisation. I know that passage of learning is still continuing for me, long after *Spirit* docked at Gisborne, the last port for Voyage 252.

Opportunities for learning came about through risk-taking. By stepping out of the boxes that we so frequently restrain ourselves within, we each discovered new things. By taking the risk of exploring and pushing ourselves outside our comfort zones and into unchartered territory, each one of us grew as a person.

For some the risk was in rolling out of our warm beds in the morning. Once the shock of the six o'clock swim had ebbed, we faced a day full of testing situations ahead of us, which generally involved the challenge of coordinating a tired body and mind to concentrate on tasks such as not spilling a plate of baked beans on another trainee. Battling seasickness and the initial fear of the unknown were the main risks taken by trainees, which continued throughout the voyage.

One of the first risks I took was to trust someone to blindfold me and guide me over the railing to the narrow outside ledge. Gripping the railing with my hands, I shuffled round the outside of the ship on my tiptoes, blind to the summer sunset but uncomfortably conscious of the fall backwards into the sea. From that moment on our comradeship and teamwork continually grew. We laughed good-naturedly as people discovered the hard way the consequences of being seasick into the wind, but scrambled to find them a cup of water and a friendly pat on the back. As we played hopscotch on the tilting deck with a spare gum-boot, two consecutive waves swamped the ship and the trainees. We clutched each other as we were washed off our feet and into the railings, and those who were already fastened to the rails held on to those who were washed into them.

In the calmer moments when anchored in a bay, we completed a ropes course from which every trainee descended and proudly displayed their shaking hands to their cheering fellow 'Spiriteers'. We swung from heights, climbed, crawled, and stretched our bodies to our limits

Female trainees climbing back on board after the 6am swim, early voyage of *Spirit of Adventure*.

and on occasion our adrenalin and *joie de vivre* ran so high as to create permanent memories of a moment. One of these was a calm summer afternoon when we paddled and surfed the waves through a cave into a hidden cove complete with a sandy beach and coral. On the way out, battling the incoming waves that were determined to push us on to the rocks, we saw a beautiful sight — *Spirit* framed by the jagged rocks that formed the high-roofed cave. All those with waterproof cameras abruptly abandoned their paddling and reached for the cameras. The rest of us struggled to stop the raft being torn to shreds on the rocks and finally we re-emerged triumphant and complete. The salt water on our hands as we gripped the sides of the raft and pushed away from the rough walls, the echoes of our group alternately yelling and laughing, still resonate in my memory. Every risk taken by the trainees, or thrown at us by the elements, nature or falling bunk beds was combated by our own determination and willingness to reach out to one another.

A section of the poem *If* by Rudyard Kipling springs to mind here:

If you can force your heart and nerve and sinew
To serve your turn long after they are gone,
And so hold on when there is nothing in you
Except the Will which says to them: 'Hold on!'

I believe all who have had the experience of sailing on either of the *Spirit* ships will have had a moment when that verse applied. Maybe it was the moment when you stood on the railing of the ship trying to force your body over the side into

Spirit of Adventure going like the clappers!

the cold sea, or a moment when seasickness ensured that your only thought was to survive that particular passage in time. All of us who shared these experiences took the risks, came through them, and are better people for stepping outside of the constraints that everyday life puts upon us. But it was so much more, because the risks we took were with other people. Together we survived the same experiences, learnt the value of the care of the people who surround us in life and depended upon the support of others to help us through those darkest hours.

My final dark hour on *Spirit*, and my moment of truth came on the last day when, encouraged by my friends, I took a deep breath and climbed to the top yardarm. Although I had spent the majority of the voyage with a thread of fear holding me back from climbing up that high, there was no question in my mind that I could allow myself to leave *Spirit* without completing this final mission. It was not purely for my own sense of achievement; it was also in memory of my grandfather who had climbed the mast of *Spirit's* sister ship, *Spirit of Adventure* when he was in his seventies. So with a feeling of determination, and a fruitless attempt to quell the butterflies in my stomach, I took my first step towards climbing the mast to the top yardarm.

I have an enduring memory of the reassuring solidity of the top yardarm pressing into my body, the untrustworthy smoothness of the wood against my palms as I was suspended there with the world at my feet. As the horizon curved before me and the sea and sky stretched as far as I could see, *Spirit* sailed on out of the bay, and my own spirit soared ahead. I know that moment will be with me until the day I die. I can still breathe in and taste the pure salt-tang air that filled my lungs, can close my eyes and see our beautiful coastline, sea and sky filling my mind. A feeling of accomplishment still surges through me and lends energy to my body. I did that. I took the risk of climbing the mast and the rewards were beyond imagining.

Can anyone now dare suggest that the risks of stepping outside our everyday lives have not been worth the results yielded, or at least the experiences and memories kept? We Spiriteers are strangers across years and across the world, but we all share one thing in common. We stepped aboard a ship and took risks. We stepped into a challenge and faced everything that was thrown our way. We each did it in our own way, but together we have shared a voyage that affects us still.

Learning to take a risk, and to celebrate my dark hours with the people around me is my legacy from the *Spirit* voyage. To risk is to make a change, to step beyond the boundaries of daily life, and to grasp an opportunity made available by the chances of this world.

To risk is more than gaining freedom, it is a liberation of self. The *Spirit* voyage, and the people that crowd my memory of those times — the crew and the voyagers — taught me that risking leads to achievement. It meant learning and discovering more about myself, about the people that fill my life as well as those that pass through my life. My voyage of self-realisation is still continuing today, long after the conclusion of the *Spirit* voyage.

BAGSHOT PARK

SPIRIT OF ADVENTURE

My brief experience of sailing on the then *Spirit of Adventure* lasted all of three days in December 1982. I was working at Wanganui Collegiate School as a House Tutor in my gap year between Gordonstoun School and Cambridge University. Overall I spent around nine months exploring New Zealand, an experience I will never forget. One of the chief highlights of that time was the opportunity to sail on *Spirit*, although I'm not sure the rest of the crew will necessarily share my sentiments.

It would be fair to say that the summer of 1982-83 was not a typical New Zealand summer; well at least not for me. For example, I spent three days walking the Milford Track in the most fantastic sunny weather, which is apparently very rare for that part of the world. I am also a member of a unique band of sailors who have been becalmed in Wellington Harbour. So when I found *Spirit* moored off Kawau Island on a beautiful sunny day with a light breeze, I thought my luck was in. It was just the sort of weather the trainees on Voyage 213 had been experiencing all week, but no sooner had we set sail than we were enveloped by a huge black cloud which deposited a large quantity of water upon us. There are no prizes for guessing who got the blame! And it didn't get much better. On day two we were forced to put a reef in and run for shelter when a full gale blew up in Tamaki Strait, reminding me more of Wellington's reputation than Auckland's.

The value of a sail-training experience can never be underestimated. There are very few, if any, truly comparable exercises which can so rapidly forge character changes, perceptions and relationships. The sea is a very humbling experience and survival, let alone making progress, depends on teamwork and trust. I learnt this on Gordonstoun's sail-training ketch *Sea Spirit*, but it was reinforced for me by watching how rapidly the trainees on Voyage 213 matured in the adverse conditions and readily took on the responsibilities of managing *Spirit* themselves on the last day.

My lasting memory of *Spirit* was the regular crew, in particular the captain Nick Hylton. His presence, stature, appearance, mannerisms and speech were ideal for running *Spirit*, and although he'll probably never forgive me for saying this, at the time I thought he would make a superb villain for a James Bond film!

Congratulations to all who have been involved in the last 30 years of providing the most fantastic opportunity for adventure and sailing for so many young New Zealanders (and a few lucky others!) through *Spirit of Adventure* and now *Spirit of New Zealand*. Good luck for the future and at least another 30 years.

HRH THE EARL OF WESSEX

A NEW START

ANDREA TOMLINSON

Andrea Tomlinson is a personal assistant to the managing director for Goldpine Industries at its Nelson head office, with responsibility for organising events, people and paper. Winner of the 2002 Topsail Award, she now sails as a watch officer on Spirit of New Zealand's day sails and has her sights set on selection as a watch officer on ten-day voyages.

IT'S JUST A BLACK BOAT with the silver fern on the side — so how and why does *Spirit of New Zealand* and everything I've experienced through her have such an impact on me as a person? Even now I still wonder this.

My first *Spirit* experience was on Voyage 169, in my sixth-form year at college. Like most teenagers, this was a time when I was searching for myself, who was I, what was I? A time when I felt lonely, useless and afraid. After ten days on the black boat, though, I had found me! The day I walked off that boat was a new start for me and a huge part of what I am today. I gained friendship, confidence, independence, self-worth, stronger communication skills, tolerance, patience and people management.

I was eager to give something back to the Trust after my voyage. I felt I wanted to give to the people who had done so much for me, and no amount of money was ever going to be enough. I became the Voyagers Club area coordinator in Nelson shortly after I finished my voyage, and held this position for six years until resigning, feeling that my National Executive duties needed to take priority. This role taught me valuable hands-on skills in dealing with people, difficult situations and time management.

After having been the area coordinator for Nelson for four years I was again struck by the magic of *Spirit*. I was encouraged by Helene Takacs, the Lower North Island representative, who made contact with me at least once a month. With her terrific support and encouragement, I was elected South Island representative on the National Executive. This position meant a lot of talking on the phone, which came naturally to me. I had my first taste of meetings, agendas, writing reports, along with the frustrations that come with working in a group with such diverse kinds of people.

After the first year on the National Exec I felt I was ready to take on a more senior role to challenge myself even more. In 2001 I took on the position of what we then called 'first mate.' The role was a new position that at times really tested me in many areas of my personality. If I thought I was challenged before, I was in for the shock of my life. Long hours, sleepless nights and countless e-mails and phone calls were all a part of my position. I strived for perfection in whatever I

Letter to Sponsor (New Zealand Company of Master Mariners), 26 June 1998

I'd like to thank you for a trip of a lifetime. The money you raised for me was fantastic. It was the best trip I have ever experienced. But the only sad thing was coming back. Because I've never met a group of kids like them. They helped me, stood up for me. And I cherish these moments in my heart.

The last day was so emotional. I made three girls cry from the story and poem I wrote and I was the only boy who made a speech straight from the heart. But to see my best friends go was really (100 x) sad. The crew members were fantastic. Sailing with a great boat, great friends, great crew members and a person like you raising money for me was tremendous.

Now I have an answer for people who only know the bad side of life. It's amazing how different people from different places change your life. I've given up smoking, drinking and tagging. I hope you know how I feel.

Thank you (100 x)

JASON LEUO
Trainee, Voyage 262, 1998

Spirit of New Zealand under full sail, including the royal sail.

did, something that often caught up on me. This role taught me so much about myself it was scary. Quickly I had to learn time management skills, leadership, people management, event organisation and the ability to adapt to change at very short notice.

To receive the Topsail Award was an honour — to think that people thought I'd done something so good it was worthy of an award. It made all my hard work seem worth while; all those hours on the phone and computer had paid off. I was probably a person who didn't make a great impact on my voyage's crew — they'd never say I was one of those 'who got a lot out of my *Spirit* trip' or learnt this, that or the other thing, but what I got out of my voyage I could never describe in words. It really changed my life and my view of life as well.

A LONG-TIME VOYAGER

JANE BETHELL

Jane Bethell has been involved with the Spirit of Adventure Trust since her ten-day voyage in 1977. She played an important role in developing the Voyagers Club and has been an active member of the Auckland Regional Association for many years. In 2003 she became the first Voyager to win the Trust's highest award, the Topgallant Award.

IT'S NOW 25 YEARS since I first became a member of the 'Spirit family'. Over that time I've been actively involved with the Trust in several ways: as a Voyager in the very early years of the Voyagers Club, as a member and committee member of the Auckland Regional Association and as national volunteer coordinator for a short time.

Spirit of Adventure and **Bounty**, 1981.

My trainee voyage on *Spirit of Adventure* was Voyage 87, an all-girl voyage in August-September 1977. I was keen to stay involved with the ship after my voyage and joined the Voyagers Club after I attended the Auckland AGM in March 1978. (For the record, I ended up on the committee!)

At that stage the Voyagers Club had been running for only a year or so, and as separate clubs out of Auckland, Wellington and Christchurch only. Even in those days, although the club was still young and social as much as anything else (particularly in Auckland), our focus was very much on staying in touch with the ship and assisting the Trust. We enjoyed each other's company and we tended to gravitate together naturally, meeting up at weekends and making trips to events like the regional boat shows.

Looking back, I think it was probably an event unrelated to Spirit that prompted us to want the Voyagers Club to be a national organisation instead of just a number of local clubs. In December 1978 a film company making a remake of *Mutiny on the Bounty* launched a replica of *Bounty* in Whangarei. Over the summer of 1978-79, Mel Bowen, Paul Leppington and Ron Bird selected and trained eleven Voyagers from around the country to crew *Bounty* for her sea trials. These Voyagers became known as the '*Bounty* Boys' (aka the '*Bounty* Babes'). Unfortunately, girls weren't allowed to take part in the sea trials, but we were determined not to be left out. With other Voyagers we spent many weekends in Whangarei the following year, working on the ship and behind the scenes. With the money raised during an Easter weekend spent crewing wharfside open days on *Bounty*, we were able to present the Trust with the carved wooden dolphins for *Spirit of Adventure*'s bows. The *Bounty* project was the perfect opportunity for us to work as a team and the Voyagers Club really took off from this time.

Encouraged by Ron Bird, Wellington and Christchurch Voyagers started local branches shortly after the Auckland branch. By 1979, with the number of ex-trainees growing by about 600 a year, many of us thought it was time to set up a National Executive to coordinate activities round the country. During the 1979 Auckland AGM, someone put forward a motion for us to bring the three branches together in a single national body. We passed the motion, stopped the Auckland AGM and started the national AGM then and there. We elected a National Executive and over the next few months worked on a written constitution. I'd been a member of the Auckland committee for several years by then and was elected as subscriptions secretary on that first National Executive. I undertook local and national committee roles for about five years in all.

Both locally and nationally we always set up our clubs as formal organisations with a chairman, secretary and treasurer, and we ran our meetings properly with formal agendas, minutes and standing rules. This has certainly benefited Voyagers who have gone on to business careers or to run other organisations.

Jane Bethell (right) with leading Auckland Regional Association volunteer Julie Oui on board *Spirit of New Zealand*.

Letter to the John Wallace McKenzie Memorial Trust. John McKenzie was one of the Spirit of Adventure Trust's founding trustees.

This is a letter expressing my thanks and gratitude for the funds and expenses that enabled me to go on Spirit of Adventure. *Your grant made it possible for me to do this. I also hope that other recipients like me will benefit from your kind generosity and funding.* (Abridged)

BEN HAUITI
Trainee, Voyage 503,
November 1996

THE FIRST FEMALE MASTER

JENNIFER ROBERTS

Jennifer Roberts has a special place in Spirit of Adventure Trust history as the first female master. Although she came from a family with no sailing background, Jennifer decided that tall ships were to be her life, and sailing as a 'chaperone' on one of the earliest girls' voyages on Spirit of Adventure *was the first step towards her goal. She now works as a marine surveyor in Tauranga.*

Your first voyage - how did it come about?

I was given a book on the Tall Ships Race across the Atlantic, a glossy picture book with fantastic photos. I remember deciding, '*That's* what I want to do.' So I figured I needed to get some experience first, which was a bit of a mission from New Zealand, but there was that *Spirit of Adventure*, she would be a good starting point... now, how to get on to that?

In 1974, Virginia Fisher was working for my father in his furniture shop, Cherrywood Furnishings, so I asked her how I should go about it. Somehow the connection was made and I was asked to do a trip as chaperone. Stan Hulford was the master and Jim Revell and Ed Danby the mates. Wisely, I think they tried to take at least one adult female on the girls' trips.

We sailed in the Hauraki Gulf that first voyage and I had a great time. I must have passed the test, as shortly after I was invited to do another trip (I think as watch officer), this time from Wellington around the Sounds, with the same crew. We had a few scary incidents, dragging anchor in the Sounds in the middle of the night, with the skipper falling down the chain locker in the middle of dealing with it. Ouch.

Shortly after, Stephen Fisher phoned me and offered me a position as permanent second mate. I was thrilled and honoured but could not accept, as I was living on Roberton Island in the Bay of Islands with Jim Cottier in those days. However, I proposed a part-time position and this was accepted. I did one trip on, two trips off, which worked satisfactorily for all parties. They transported me to Auckland too, sometimes by bus, but often by SeeBee Air, with the amphibian collecting me direct from the beach on the island. What fun!

What tickets had you achieved by then?

I'd acquired a restricted limits licence by this stage. I'd started working at Fullers Ferries to earn pocket money over the summer break when we had to vacate the island for the owner, and had quickly figured it was a better job driving the boats than working as deckhand: cleaning toilets, emptying the ashtrays and mopping up spew. A qualification was obviously the way to a better job! And so began the chase for sea time, a chase which lasted for the next twenty-odd years.

I progressed quickly through the ranks, getting to mate with the huge support of Captain Nick Hylton, without whom none of this would have happened.

Some time after that I went overseas to follow my dreams and spent eighteen months on the Norwegian fully rigged ship *Sorlandet*. I took with me a nice letter of recommendation from Bob Lawry, who was then running the Spirit of Adventure office. When I came back, I had enough sea time to sit for second mate foreign going and immediately after that I was promoted to master.

That must have been a special moment?

I felt very proud on my first trip as master. We sailed out and had to swing the compass before leaving. We must have had the compass adjuster on board. I flew the correct code flags for 'I am adjusting my compasses' and heard later that there had been a very critical gathering of mariners in the cafeteria of the nautical school who were watching and laughing at the odd flags flying — what a fool of a girl, what does she think she is doing, turning left instead of right, doesn't she know the way out of the harbour, etc. Then one of them went off to look up the flags. Apparently they went a bit quiet when they found out what the code flags meant. Sam Jackson, a great stalwart volunteer, related all this to me. He was one of my big fans and took great delight in telling me the story.

I felt I had 'done my time' on *Spirit* and

Master Jennifer Roberts at the helm of *Spirit of Adventure*.

Letter to sponsor (Formica New Zealand Limited), 29 October 1986

I've learnt, like most other trainees, that a voyage on Spirit *is not all fun and games. It takes personal strength, perseverance and sometimes patience to last ten days on a sailing ship at sea with 36 trainees on board. I've learnt how to live in a very small space with a lot of other people and we've all learnt that, if we work together as a team, tasks are completed easily and very quickly.* (Abridged)
BRIDGETTE ADLAM
Trainee, Voyage 6
(*Spirit of New Zealand*)

felt ready to take command. It was of course stressful at times, but overall I enjoyed it immensely. With my teaching background and extensive sailing experience, I felt the work on *Spirit* nicely combined my two strengths.

I enjoyed the company of the male crew — people passionate about square-rig like trustee John Duder, who was one of my early second mates. He did a trip when there were only two males on board, John and the engineer, Jim Pretty. The worst ones were the macho firemen volunteers, who were not too happy about having a female in charge. However, many of them I soon won over, and they became very supportive. A few resisted and I was happy not to have to sail with them again. These days I could cope better with them than I did then. I was probably pretty confident about my sailing abilities and just tried to ignore the doubters. I set high standards for myself and for all my crew.

The trainees were treated all the same, boys and girls, although we all enjoyed the girls' trips more. The girls were easier to control and were more fun too.

Do you think a female master would be regarded differently now?

I think that then I was a strong role model for the girls. I always told them that they could do anything they set their minds to do, so hopefully helped to inspire a large number of girls to strive for their dreams.

These days it's more common to have women in leading roles. It would not be as 'shocking' as it must have been then. I was largely blissfully unaware of their reactions — I had to ignore all of that, and concentrate on doing a good job. I believed that I had to be better than the blokes to be accepted and I worked very hard to succeed. The kids would most likely be more accepting of a female master today, having been exposed to all the females in high places recently.

I had no female role models. Nick Hylton and my partner Jim Cottier, a master mariner, were really my best role models and I tried hard to follow their good examples. I thought of myself as a trailblazer and, as one of the few female marine surveyors around, still do. Sometimes I ask myself why I always seem to be swimming upstream, against the flow.

I don't know if the male trainees behaved any differently towards me than they would have towards a male captain. I never considered the possibility. A certain arrogance, perhaps, but more likely a protective mechanism...

I had problems with a few trainees, but nothing remarkable. My early teaching background stood me in good stead for handling teenagers. I always had a good team with me. In those days, the Trust managed to provide many experienced mates to back up the new masters. My seamanship did not seem to be a problem. With all the sailing I had done over the years, I had a huge background of experience.

Was there a special rapport between the female crew?

Yes, I had great support from the other females behind me. I keep in touch with many of them. In fact, all of my best friends are ex-*Spirit* crew. We often get together and sometimes tell stories from *Spirit* days. The friends you make at sea are usually lifelong friends. Something to do with sharing the best and worst of life at close quarters, I guess.

What were the differences between the girls' trips and the boys' trips?

The girls were nicer, cleaner, better behaved, more easily controlled and used less bad language. All the crew agreed that girls' trips were better. The girls also appreciated the experience more and seemed to get more out of it. Especially in the early days, it was quite a special thing for them to be able to go sailing and they really got a huge kick out of it. That made it more rewarding for us too.

Yes, I really enjoyed dealing with 25 young people. I didn't enjoy it so much when we got *Spirit of New Zealand* with its larger numbers. It lost the intimacy and personal attention you could give the kids. I didn't enjoy the mixed trips as much either.

I started out on the *Spirit*s, as did most of the crew, for my own benefit — to get some experience so I could get on to the big square-riggers, but ended up being there for the kids. I think that happened to most people. It was the single biggest and best thing that ever happened to me, working on *Spirit*. It changed my life, from being a self-centred seafarer to giving something back.

And the main changes you saw in the kids?

Confidence mainly. Especially in the girls.

Sublime moments?

Too many to have one stand out. Drifting under square rig on a lovely starry night is very special, but perhaps I got spoiled with many sublime times like that.

A highlight of my career was sailing as 'commodore' on *Spirit of New Zealand* for the 1990 Sesquicentennial celebrations, in charge of a small fleet of square-rigged vessels: *Spirit of Adventure, Spirit of New Zealand, Breeze, R Tucker Thompson, Tradewind* and *Young Endeavour* from Australia.

The team on *Young Endeavour* were very hospitable and made me a commodore's flag out of a pillow slip. They hoisted the flag whenever I stepped on board *Young Endeavour*. I still have the flag, which I treasure.

CAPTAIN FRENCH AGENT

On one particular 'white ship' voyage, we were peacefully at anchor at day's end. It was a time when the *Rainbow Warrior* episode was still fresh in our minds. The captain was pursuing his hobby of scuba diving, while the lady first officer was discussing the day's events with the trainees on the afterdeck. Unnoticed by the group, a pair of hands came over the coaming and gradually made their way aft until they were opposite the wheel. Suddenly, with a flurry, the top half of a wetsuit and an air bottle appeared above the deck. A male voice called cheerfully, 'Bonjour, mademoiselle.' The discussion group scattered in disarray.

BRUCE LETHBRIDGE
Volunteer crew

A FAMILY AFFAIR

SHEILA BUGDEN

Sheila Budgen, a Nelson podiatrist, and her pharmacist husband Chris
typify the 'Spirit volunteer family.' With little background in sailing
(Chris once owned a Sunburst), they listened to daughter Nicola's stories
of her trainee voyage, and determined to 'give it a go' themselves.

OUR FAMILY'S involvement with the Spirit of Adventure Trust began with our daughter Nicola's voyage on *Spirit of Adventure* in 1985. Voyage 264 had an unexpected end. The day the ship should have arrived in Wanganui we received a phone call from the office in Auckland telling us not to worry, everyone was safe, but the ship would be a day late and arriving in New Plymouth instead. *Spirit of Adventure* had encountered a storm in Cook Strait and the master had judged it too rough to attempt to cross the sometimes dangerous bar off Wanganui.

Knowing then very little about the work of the Trust, we happily accepted the explanation. From our current involvement, I can now appreciate the chaos this must have caused at the office, with the trainees and crew in the wrong port and needing altered travel plans, the ship in the wrong place for the next voyage, and Wanganui's plans to celebrate the ship's visit made suddenly redundant.

As with all trainees, our daughter came back with great stories of all her experiences on the ship, and we realised she had been part of something very special. We promptly joined up as supporters of the Trust so that we'd be able to nominate our other children in turn, and they too would be able to experience the Spirit magic. Unfortunately our second daughter Sarah was quite sick at the time that she would have sailed and didn't have the chance to do a voyage, but our son Tim did his on *Spirit of New Zealand* in 1988 on Voyage 42.

In 1994 *Spirit of New Zealand* was in Nelson and my husband and I did a half-day sail to see for ourselves something of the experience that had been so memorable for Nicola and Tim. As a result of that sail, Chris decided to sign on for a six-day adult coastal voyage from Wellington to Auckland.

Despite the rough passage from Wellington up the Wairarapa coast, he thoroughly enjoyed the voyage and was captivated by the experience of being at the helm on a starlit night with just the sound of the waves and the sight of phosphorescent dolphins, like torpedoes, swimming alongside the ship. Once back home he applied to join the volunteer crew. I rashly offered to help if the ship was in port and so, when *Spirit* returned the following year, I was co-opted as 'secretary' for the Nelson sub-region. Having a fear of heights, a dislike of deep water and no experience of sailing, I had no intention of doing anything other than shore-based jobs.

A trainee helps to raise the mainsail on *Spirit of New Zealand.*

In 1996 I was persuaded to try an adult coastal voyage from Dunedin to Bluff on *Spirit of Adventure*. Steve Gamble, famous in the organisation as the first trainee to return as a professional skipper, was master, and Captain Tom Sawyer the first mate. With such leadership, who could fail to be captivated by the Spirit organisation and the people involved?

In 1997 Chris and I went to Auckland for the annual general meeting and decommissioning of *Spirit of Adventure* and following that weekend I sailed out, with much trepidation, on *Spirit of New Zealand* as a watch leader. Having Tom Sawyer as master and Mel Pearson as a fellow watch leader was a potent combination for a first voyage. I remember watching Tom, with perfectly straight face, explaining to the trainees at the 8 am ritual of raising the colours that Great Barrier Island, being volcanic, was made of pumice and therefore floated on very high tides, so it would be necessary for us to check its position when we got close. What an education they and I had in ten days!

Just like the trainees, I discovered I could do all sorts of things if I just gave them a go. I've been involved in some amazing activities during the various voyages I've crewed on. 'You expect me to swim from ship to shore, Jim? You are joking!' He was not! 'You want me to *jog* across Kawau Island? Me, jog, you are kidding!' He was not! There have been many times — like climbing the rigging in the dark with a crew member, with a bucket full of water balloons in a pack on my back to tuck in the topsail — when I've seriously wondered whether this was a suitable activity for a grandma! But why not?

On a CanTeen trip (CanTeen is an organisation for teenagers with cancer, and their siblings), we made origami boats and wrote on them the names of friends we wanted to remember who'd died of cancer. On a beautiful starry night off Torrent Bay, in the Abel Tasman National Park, we dropped the little boats over the side into the sea. On a disabled sail, I was greatly impressed by a member of my watch with cerebral palsy who couldn't swim but who really wanted to be part of the morning routine. Wearing a buoyancy aid and with her buddy in the water ready to catch her, she leaped confidently over the side and was helped back on to the ship with eyes shining and a look of satisfaction that remains a treasured memory.

We've had great times with Warick Biggs, the Nelson port contact and the Nelson members. Until 2002 Nelson was a sub-region of Wellington, which we found unwieldy. Since then we've become a region in our own right, and we intend to continue as before with Warick officially as chairman.

Once we know the ship's schedule, we start the process of deciding what to do when *Spirit of New Zealand* comes to Nelson. The length of time the ship is in port and the time of year dictate the various options. It's good to offer the public an overnight sail, especially with the Abel Tasman National Park so accessible from Port Nelson. Unfortunately that option requires limited numbers of crew and some of our members are only available for day sails. We also like to give as many local Voyagers as possible the chance to come back and help crew.

My son Tim has just returned from his voyage (No. 533) and, wow, he has really enjoyed himself. His confidence seems to have grown over the past 12 days and I'm sure we owe a lot of that to the way you people organise things for these kids. We were very impressed right from the time we received our pre-sail mail. Many thanks also to your very patient telephone operator who received several phone calls from one panicky mother! Tim had never been on any public transport before (except a school bus!). He thoroughly enjoyed his experience and has a lot of new friends.

Many thanks for a well-organised and enjoyable endeavour for New Zealand's youth. This is something Tim will remember all his life and we thank you all most sincerely from the bottom of our hearts for something that is so positive for our New Zealand youth.

(Abridged)

ROSE BAIGENT
Parent of trainee

Spirit of New Zealand under full sail

We are always grateful for the support we get from various sources when *Spirit* is in port. The majority of incoming trainees for a ten-day voyage usually arrive by Intercity bus and, after the rest of the passengers have disembarked at the bus depot, the bus company does an extra trip to drop the incoming trainees off at the wharf. Similarly, when the trainees leave the ship, rather than having to organise transport for them all into town, the bus comes to pick them up at the wharf. Port Nelson helps us with advertising the ship's visit and ensures that port costs to us are kept to a minimum; Sport Tasman provides a base for our ticket sales. For the last couple of years we have held a raffle on each sail — a plastic bag from the Two Dollar Shop filled with local 'goodies' — and local businesses, wineries and producers of all sorts have donated wonderful things to put in the bags.

When *Spirit of New Zealand* came to Nelson in October 2002 we did a special afternoon sail for those who have supported us locally in different ways. We thought it would be nice to give something back to our community. We had many grateful comments from those sailing and, having had the mayor of Nelson on board, were delighted when the next council meeting voted $2000 annually to be set aside for youngsters to apply to for voyage funding.

We've had some interesting and varied day sails out of Nelson. Cyclone Drena swept through one January causing our Saturday sailings to be cancelled and the Sunday sailings to be shortened due to the rough seas. We've had a wedding on board, with the crew lining up to form a guard of honour for the bride as she boarded the ship. During another visit we did a day sail for disabled people. Nelson's Seafarers Memorial Trust was launched during a special evening sail on *Spirit*, when a model of a 2-metre bronze statue they hoped to erect on a new wharf on Nelson's Wakefield Quay was unveiled. Since then that Trust has used an evening sail on *Spirit* on every visit to Nelson for further fundraising, and they acknowledge our part in getting the wharf and statue finally in place in 2001. Each year, we're invited to take part in their 'Blessing of the Hoki Fleet' service.

For the Year of the Older Person in 1999 we organised sails for local rest home residents. I think Nelson still holds the record for having the oldest sailor on board. Mrs Davies was 104 and, sitting on a chair brought on deck from the crew mess, was thrilled to pull on a rope to help hoist a sail. Whilst the Spirit programme is designed for youth development, I don't think we will forget the joyful tears and appreciation expressed by so many of the older folk that they too had been able to share a special experience.

VOMITOLOGY ...
OR A TREATISE ON REVERSE PERISTALSIS

TOM SAWYER

Captain Tom Sawyer joined the Volunteer Crew Association in the early 1980s. He worked his way up through the ranks from watch leader through navigator and other roles to his present position of relieving master. Tom has been port contact for Bluff since about 1985 and received the Spirit of Adventure Trust's Topgallant Award in 1999. He lives in Invercargill, where he has a shipping agency.

IN THE SIXTH CENTURY BC the Greek philosopher Anarchasis, when asked whether there were more people living than dead, replied, 'In which group do I put those sailing on the sea?'

In 55BC Julius Caesar and his horses were violently seasick during their journey across the English Channel to invade England. The situation has not improved since then!

While no sail-training ship master would deliberately set out to make the crew or trainees sick, there are often times when circumstances make a certain amount of *mal de mer* inevitable. There are two stages of seasickness. The first, which is bad, is when you know you are going to die. The second stage, which is far worse, is when you realise that you are not.

Now, for all the bad points about seasickness, it does have some good ones: first, the attendant humour (of which more later), secondly, the fact that, in this increasingly 'green' age, it's 100% biodegradable, and thirdly, the levelling effect. There is nothing quite so good at bringing trainees on to a metaphorical 'level playing-field' than seasickness. It's very hard to think of yourself as superior when you are lying in a pool of vomit along with your fellows. And as a member of the first fifteen, or head prefect or whatever (and it's always the boys!), it's no use gritting your teeth and being macho about the whole thing. The stomach always wins and the double stream from the nostrils always brings tears to the eyes of the beholders, let alone the trainee doing the vomiting.

Every trip brings its own stories as trainees give of their all to win the 'Chunderthon Trophy'. These stories, the sharing of a difficult experience, are part of the process of bringing the trainees of each voyage together as a team. Occasionally it involves a selfless act of sheer valour and caring for one's shipmates, as in the case of the young watch officer in Foveaux Strait. Aloft on the course yard, this fine fellow pulled out the front of his boiler suit to vomit into, rather than drop the lot on the trainees below.

More often, it's the sense of humour and the resilience of youth that make for unforgettable moments. We're up the Wairarapa coast, Wellington to Napier, in a big southerly roll. Seasick trainees are scattered about and there's a couple on death row. A Maori lass called Lee is matching Pakeha Mike chunder for chunder. Following a sterling effort from Lee that almost turns her inside out, Mike was heard to say, 'I don't suppose you want your fishing quota now, do you Lee?'

Same coast, different trip and a small trainee called Sam is giving his all over the rail. 'Got a weak stomach there, Sam?' was the question. Quick as a flash came back the answer: 'No sir, I can throw it as far as anybody else!'

It's this attitude, this spark of fun in the face of adversity, that makes the crew realise the strength and resilience that our young people have. In this modern, often pampered, world there are many times when, even if one has a problem, it can be walked away from. Seasickness is different. It is apparently serious, it hurts and you can't just walk away from it. You face it and beat it yourself.

The experience of doing this, of beating something apparently unbeatable, raises the self-esteem and the self-confidence of a young trainee like few other experiences they will ever come across.

Developing youth at sea! Heavy weather on *Spirit of New Zealand*.

AN EXCELLENT APPRENTICESHIP

MARGARET PIDGEON

Margaret Pidgeon, Australian-born, was one of a group of talented women who sailed with the Spirit of Adventure Trust during the early 1980s and went on to notable careers as professional seafarers. Promoted to her first merchant command in 1997, Margaret wrote these recollections of her early Spirit training while in command of MS Aotearoa Chief, *a 130-metre (about 10,500 tonne DWT) container ship, steaming from Rabaul, Papua New Guinea to Chuuk, Federated States of Micronesia with an all-Chinese crew, except chief and second engineers.*

BY THE TIME I became involved in the Spirit organisation in the early eighties, women and girls were a well-accepted part of the team. Female trainees had been sailing since Voyage 11 in 1974, and women as mates had become commonplace. However, for me those first trips were still a huge eye-opener. Having hardly been on a boat of any kind before, I had no idea what to expect or how anything worked, so my watch and I muddled through, having great fun and eventually learning from our many mistakes.

Fortunately, Captain Nick Hylton seemed to have endless patience. By the end of my first trip in 1980 in the Hauraki Gulf, I had the bug. There was a great feeling of camaraderie and excitement, and in my case the satisfaction of learning a great deal very quickly, as I threw myself into the whole programme. Everyone was expected to do their personal best, and we all did it because we could see that the Spirit experience was such a good thing for the trainees. I think what kept us all coming back was the excellent feedback from so many of the trainees — and it was great fun!

I quickly slotted into the Spirit family, which included quite a few strong and interesting women. They were all role models in different ways, and many also became friends.

It was not until a few years later that I heard about tickets and seatime. Again, I just followed the crowd — it was reasonably normal for females to go off to nautical school by that stage. I'd realised that I really did want to be able to get a permanent job on *Spirit*, and to do that, I needed the piece of paper. The Trust had been an equal-opportunity employer for a long time before I joined, and I greatly benefited from that attitude, probably without realising it at the time. Looking back, I gained great confidence from the Spirit of Adventure Trust's attitude that, with proper training, most people would be able to realise their ambitions. I did not feel that I had to fight any great equality battles — becoming competent was enough. I don't remember consciously thinking that I wanted to become captain. It was very much a case of one step at a time and let's see where it takes me.

Three trainees in heavy weather gear, early girls' voyage on *Spirit of Adventure*, January 1977.

When I became permanent mate in 1983, I was really aware of not letting the side down for other women, past, present and future. My predecessors — Jennifer Roberts, Grae Glieu, Naomi Petersen, Heidi Richardson and Elizabeth England — had set very high standards, and I tried hard to maintain them. I also felt very strongly (and still do) that it was really important that, as women, we just got on and did things, without making a big song and dance about it and without expecting any special treatment. I think (hope?) that this attitude rubbed off on the trainees, especially the young women. I can't remember many instances of discrimination for simply being female. In fact, I felt that sometimes there was a bit of reverse discrimination (and maybe some of the males felt this too), but perhaps this was only an attempt to redress the balance after so many years of the opposite.

I was fortunate to be with the Spirit of Adventure Trust during a really exciting period. There was a great deal happening with the southern voyages and the building of *Spirit of New Zealand*. Being part of the building team was exhilarating but also exhausting; the job list never seemed to get any smaller, no matter how hard we all worked!

The input from the volunteers was and remains immense, bringing a wide range of skills and experience, plus fresh energy and enthusiasm. I feel they are a big part of why the Spirit of Adventure Trust has remained so successful. Volunteers helped us to keep our standards high. The Trust was generally well respected for the way it did things and we were all aware of the importance of our public image. Volunteers also helped prevent the permanent crew from becoming 'stale'. It is very different in merchant ships where there is usually only a small number of officers and crew, and often the same people for months on end.

The first few mixed trips in *Spirit of New Zealand* following her commissioning in 1986 produced some innovative solutions to the perennial problem of getting 40 exuberant trainees to calm down and go to bed for the night. I think it was Nick Hylton in *Spirit of Adventure* who first introduced the idea of the very long, boring lectures late at night, which generally succeeded in putting most of the trainees (and some officers) to sleep. In *Spirit of New Zealand*, we discovered another trick — the aft cabin skylights. Once all were assembled in the aft cabin, and when it was nearly time for lights out, one of the officers would quietly close all the skylights from above, while the lecturer droned on — it never failed.

One of my proudest moments in *Spirit of New Zealand* was the day before the start of the Tall Ships Race in January 1988 in Hobart. As per our usual programme, we had a completely new bunch of trainees, in this instance joining on the day before the start of the race, fresh from their flight from New Zealand. Of course, most of them had absolutely no sailing experience, so we went out for a day's intensive sail training. All went pretty well for a first day, and the other mate, Steve Gamble, and I were starting to relax a little before returning back alongside.

Spirit of New Zealand in Hobart Harbour following the Tall Ships Race which was part of the Australian Bicentennial celebrations in January 1988.

Then we realised that Nick Hylton was not calling for all sail to be handed, he was just reducing to working rig and sailing in slowly towards the crowded dock. A quick look at Nick's face told me that we had better get this one right or we would become a permanent fixture under the bowsprit of US Coastguard ship *Eagle*, which was occupying the berth ahead of us. So with what felt like all of the sailors in Hobart watching, not to mention the duty watch on *Eagle* peering down on us, we 'sailed' alongside. The trainees did really well, with the foredeck and midships teams managing to drop the sails correctly. We got the spring out smartly and stopped perfectly in position — what an absolute buzz! Of course the main engine was ticking over and yes, I think Nick did give a small touch of the engine astern and maybe a bit of a squirt on the bow thruster, but it was not obvious to most onlookers. The trainees had no idea why all the officers were grinning so broadly, as all had been done with hardly a word spoken.

While we were making fast, an old man stepped out of the crowd and threw a small object at the ship. I happened to look up just in time to catch an Australian penny. What a surprise when I saw that it was for 1952 — the year of my birth. It's been my lucky penny ever since and I always take it to sea with me. Who says sailors aren't superstitious?!

One night in Sydney later in the same voyage, giving the trainees the briefing for the next day, I concluded with the fateful statement, 'You're all old enough to know the right thing to do, so we are not going to set a curfew tonight. We will see all of you at the 0600 PT and run (no swim as we're inside the harbour).'

The next morning, there was one newly shaved head, several pierced ears and quite a few headaches (no tattoos that I saw!), but to their credit they were all there on deck on time, ready to run. I was more careful with how I worded things after that.

I was lucky enough to participate in Voyage 165 of Spirit of New Zealand *from Napier to Wellington.*

I got so much out of my voyage. As well as learning how to sail a big ship and all about nautical things … I also learnt a lot about myself — my personality and how I relate to others. There were opportunities to participate in leadership and teamwork activities and to try so many new challenges. I was so proud of myself when I climbed the rigging.

It seems a pity that every young New Zealander cannot take part in one of these voyages as there is so much to gain, but it is wonderful that so many people have. I thank you once more for the opportunities that you made available to me and to thousands of others. It was great.

(Abridged)

Fiona Robinson
Trainee, Voyage 165, 1993

It is well documented that *Spirit* sea-going staff suffer from burnout and I was no exception. After the excitement of being part of the building and learning to run the bigger, more challenging *Spirit of New Zealand*, and the Tall Ships event in Australia, I was ready to move on.

Continuing a life at sea appealed and I thought I would like to try for more qualifications — the next step was a foreign-going certificate. So after a long 'apprenticeship', I finally completed the required seatime and passed second mate foreign-going in 1989.

Due to the merchant shipping company (Swire's) extreme shortage of junior officers at the time, I managed to get a job with Swire Pacific Ship Management in 1989. I joined MS *Hunan* from a 'bum' boat in Singapore Strait in the middle of the night: the learning curve was the same as the pilot ladder stretching up the ship's side — vertical.

My sail-training background, with its emphasis on sharing knowledge freely and facilitating discovery learning, had not prepared me for the harsh commercial reality of a trading vessel. I went from being a 'big fish' in the Spirit pond to nearly the lowest deck officer (3/0), who obviously didn't have a clue about anything. Even the cadets seemed to know more than me — at least in the beginning.

However, eventually I learnt how to do cargo watches and ballasting and all the various duties of a merchant officer. After the busy *Spirit* days, I enjoyed the quiet solitude of bridge watches with only a sole AB as lookout for company. And the luxury of being off watch and knowing that you wouldn't be called unless for emergencies. Careers in the merchant navy follow a well-defined path, and once I managed to get one foot on the bottom of the ladder, it was a normal, logical progression to my becoming captain of MS *Chengtu* in 1997.

When I came to New Zealand as master of MS *Coral Chief* for the first time in January 1999, it was a great feeling of solidarity to have Jennifer Roberts as the cargo surveyor at Mount Maunganui, Joanne Stanley as our pilot in Lyttelton, and Kim Peny at the Maritime Safety Authority in Wellington. There were many phone calls and e-mails - not all strictly business. New Zealand is probably unusual in this regard, having quite a few women employed in various capacities at sea and in related fields ashore. Worldwide, I have yet to meet another female serving as captain of a merchant ship, although I have met four female pilots, two in USA, one in Australia and Joanne in Lyttelton.

'Where did you serve your time?' is the classic question asked of one seafarer by another. I'm always proud to reply that I served some of my time with *Spirit* and also in the small trading scow *Te Aroha* on the Great Barrier Island run. It was not until after I left the Spirit of Adventure Trust that I realised our standards were quite high. *Spirit* provided a broad apprenticeship in seamanship which, unfortunately, is generally lacking in merchant ships today. The Trust also gave many women their big break in getting into a sea-going career.

THE BEST OF TIMES...

TONY COOPER

Tony Cooper of Picton began his family's 20-year association with the Spirit of Adventure *Trust as a paying passenger on* Spirit of Adventure. *This Hauraki Gulf voyage in 1982 was to be the first of many by all the members of his family, and the start of a long and ongoing association with the Trust.*

IN 1982 A FRIEND told me about a sailing trip undertaken by one of his friends on a small sailing ship called *Spirit of Adventure*. I'd done some sailing before emigrating to New Zealand in 1974 and I knew a bit about the English sail training ship *Sir Winston Churchill* so I asked, 'What do you have to do to get on the *Spirit*?'

'Just ring this number, they will send you a list of available trips, pay your money and you're on.'

This was simple enough even for me. I was then running my own engineering business, so I didn't have to ask for time off from the boss, only from my wife Sue, which was granted.

The paperwork done and money paid (I can't recall the cost), my first 'adult voyage' was five days, Auckland to Auckland. When the appointed day came, we decided to make the trip to Auckland a family affair. While I was away sailing, Sue and our three children spent the time around the attractions of the city. We lived near Bulls then, so there was much to do and see.

The skipper on that voyage was Nick Hylton; many will remember him, his smelly old pipe and laid-back, friendly disposition. We visited Little Barrier Island, where the ranger came on board to give us a talk about the island before we all went ashore for a walk. I found over the following years that this sort of rare opportunity would come several times.

My log book shows I did four paid voyages until someone from the permanent crew suggested I join the volunteer crew. Then I could be part of the Spirit team for free, and lead a watch. We were called fourth and third mates in those days. Ironically, while these titles sounded a bit grand, I know they meant very little to non-maritime people, whereas today's watch leader title means something to most people.

Sue's records show she first sailed on a weekend voyage as a paying passenger. She wasn't happy on deck pulling on ropes and climbing masts but she wanted to be involved. An easy and important way for her to do this on subsequent voyages was to be the cook. Since sailing as assistant cook on Voyage 135A from Wellington to Napier, Sue has sailed many times as cook. One of my favourite images is of Sue trying to persuade the troops to partake of some porridge halfway

Thank you for the marvellous work you do with your youth programme. Two of our children have taken part and they both gained so much from the experience — particularly our son whose confidence and self-esteem improved so greatly during his time on Spirit of New Zealand.
(Abridged)
SAM WALKER AND FAMILY, 1996
Parents of trainee

across Cook Strait in a stiff breeze (howling gale to Aucklanders). Needless to say, most were too busy studying the horizon.

It was quite difficult being allocated a sailing position in the early nineties because there were plenty of good people keen to sail and doing good service as watch leaders. The Wellington Volunteer Crew Association was particularly enthusiastic and played its part in showing Auckland how to fill the ships on weekends.

Around this time we appointed ourselves the Bulls branch of the Spirit organisation. We would book *Spirit of Adventure* by putting the deposit, a quarter of the total weekend price of about $7000, on our credit card, and set about finding enough punters to pay us a deposit to cover this. After several weeks collecting crew and money together, we would invite everyone to our place for a pot luck dinner where we would tell people what to expect, what to bring.

I also managed to persuade the Auckland office to use volunteer crew from Palmerston North and Wellington; many of these came to the dinners. This approach meant that most of the punters had met each other and some of the crew before we boarded the ship. Consequently, the weekends went very well and we made many good friends at the same time.

Sue and I did about ten of these voyages, including one monumental mission for a three-day weekend on *Spirit of New Zealand.* Con Thode was the master, and how could we forget mate John Duder and his crew capsizing a whaler? Friends still remember the incident with pleasure. I was the rescuer in the 'tinny' and can still see some of the crew sitting on the upturned whaler. No one was upset by the experience, which we all put down to being part of a great weekend adventure.

Most of the voyages we organised were Wellington to Wellington. We would usually 'heave' our way across Cook Strait, with many of the punters, whom I usually referred to as 'paying victims', only coming to life when we entered the Tory Channel. We witnessed many acts of bravery and compassion despite the ship rolling so much as to send half its complement to the lee rail; for example, a lady asking a gentleman, who was himself in a very sad state, if he would hold her false teeth so she wouldn't lose them. It never ceased to amaze me how much purgatory we would all suffer and still come back for more — selective memory, I guess. Ivor Saunders from the Wellington VCA and I would convince each other we were *not* coming back again, until the next time.

On another occasion we 'lost' granny Coleman, an elderly lady well in her eighties. She was found asleep in the safety nets under the bowsprit. One visit to Port Underwood in the early days of *Spirit of New Zealand* saw us leaving with a huge sack of mussels given us by a local. On one Wellington day sail, my eighty-year-old mum got to steer the ship, a memory she cherishes. Such memories as these endure, and I'm sure provide us all, punters, trainees and crew, with memories to last forever.

Sue and I decided to make *Spirit* compulsory enjoyment for our three children as they became old enough and could find half the money for their fees. Roger was the first, and lucky enough to be picked for the Melbourne to Hobart leg on *Spirit of New Zealand* for the 1988 Bicentenary celebrations in Australia. The Rotary Club of Launceston hosted them, and the president wrote to me (I was a Rotarian at the time) to congratulate us on our boy and the whole crew, saying what a wonderful bunch of youngsters they were.

Rog went on to sail as leading hand and as a buddy with the disabled voyages. When he came back from overseas many years later he sailed as volunteer cook, then went on to join the permanent crew as cook, then on deck as second mate. He even met his fiancée, Liz Clark, on *Spirit of New Zealand* when she sailed as a watch leader.

Next was Pam. I remember phoning Pippa Tizzard in the Auckland office to see if there were any berths available in the near future. There were some out of Wellington but I chose Bluff to Dunedin, Voyage 128, as it was farthest away. Our contribution to the fee was Pam's sixteenth birthday present. As the sailing date drew nearer, she became less enthusiastic about going and flew out of Palmerston North looking rather glum.

I remember with some pride a very different young woman stepping off the plane on her return. Admitting that once she realised that everything on the ship had to be cleaned for everyone's benefit, she then set to and made the most of the adventure, as do most of the trainees.

Pam went on to sail as a buddy and help out on day sails in Wellington, also encouraging her husband Glen to take part. The next will be their son Evan, though at three years old he has a little way to go yet.

Next in line was Nigel. He had done a couple of day sails and at least one weekend voyage, as well as his ten-day experience on Voyage 215, in April 1996. Nigel enjoyed this voyage and went on to be a leading hand and a buddy on a disabled voyage.

Leaving school later in 1996 to work as a kayak guide near Lake Taupo, Nigel applied to the Trust for the position of cadet and was accepted. He started in April 1997, and this first voyage in uniform was captured in the photo (above) by John Curruthers, a friend from Palmerston North who was sailing as a watch leader. Nigel enjoyed his cadetship immensely. His fellow cadets were Amanda Slee, who is now second mate with the Interislander, and Alistair Campbell from Taupo.

The cadets were unpaid, so part of the challenge for him and us was funding. We were amazed by the attitude of the employment people, who would pay the unemployment benefit to everyone except Spirit of Adventure Trust cadets. Their rationale was that he had a 'job' even though it was unpaid. Student loans were unavailable for cadets, because they did not fit into the appropriate slots in the

Former *Spirit of New Zealand* cadet Nigel Cooper (14 June 1979 - 21 May 1999).

The Spirit of Adventure Trust farewelled Nigel Cooper in a short ceremony of remembrance on board Spirit of New Zealand *in May 1999 in the Bay of Islands. Nigel was a keen writer of verse. He wrote this piece several months before his death.*

OCEANS

There are things in this world which shall never be told,
Things close to the heart and closed inside the mind,
A person's heart is a deep ocean with much to reveal and much more to hide.
The depths of this ocean pass beyond our comprehension into areas of grey
With things which shall never be told and be boxed away forever.
For no one person can ever know everything about a person
If that one does not know themselves how to cross their own ocean limits and
Reveal the depths for their own mind.

NIGEL COOPER
2 March 1999

system. Then someone advised Nigel to tell the Palmerston North employment people that he wanted a job as a deckhand on a foreign-going ship. This was great. They could put him in a slot. He had to front up regularly for an interview, but we managed to get around this by saying he was doing voluntary work and would not be back for ten days or so. Sometimes they assumed I was Nigel (on the phone) and they were happy with a chat. This system worked pretty well for most of his cadetship, and with a bit of help from us and his friends he survived financially.

For his 'launch time' he went to Gisborne for a couple of months to work on tugs, staying with Peter and Barbara Pole. Many of the friends he made during his cadetship still keep in contact with us.

From Gisborne Nigel joined the Interisland Line and spent a season working on the *Condor 10* fast ferry as 'ordinary seaman'. Accepted as a trainee deck officer, he joined the ferry *Arahura* in May 1999. The rest, as they say, is history. Nigel was killed in a stupid and tragic accident during a rescue boat drill on 21 May 1999. A promising career came to an end.

Subsequently we bought a yacht in Nigel's name and set up a trust which we plan will help our grandchildren participate in the sort of things that their late uncle loved.

During the negotiations to put *Waianawa* into charter in Picton, we ended up buying the company Charterlink Marlborough. So we now live in Picton and are still involved with the Spirit of Adventure Trust as port contacts. We have taken sick trainees off the ship, put late ones on, and usually go on board to deliver spares and have a coffee and catch up with old friends. Sue also occasionally sails as cook.

Our *Spirit* lives have had many highlights. Many years ago I was talked into being a Coastguard education tutor by Sarah Watchman, something I still enjoy doing. I was able to sail as watch leader on Nigel's last voyage, and several disabled and leader manager courses. I sailed on *Spirit of Adventure* on the offshore voyage to beat them all, to Raoul Island in the Kermadecs and back, a totally unforgettable experience, and I was crew for *Spirit* master Jim Dilley and partner Tori on their voyage to Tonga in their yacht *Erenya*.

We have seen so many people, young and old, gain so much from their unique experience on board both *Spirit of Adventure* and *Spirit of New Zealand*, none more than Sue, Roger, Pam, Nigel and myself.

TO BE WHO YOU WANT TO BE

ANNETTE CULPAN

In November 2002 Annette Culpan's employer, Vodafone New Zealand, sent her on a ten-day voyage on Spirit of New Zealand. *As a sponsor of the Spirit of Adventure Trust, Vodafone had secured a berth on each of ten consecutive voyages. Annette's role on Voyage 385 was as assistant watch leader and mentor for the ten teenagers placed in her watch.*

THE FIRST THING that strikes you about *Spirit of New Zealand* is her size and immense beauty. She appeared to me to be something very grand out of a history book — an ominous, complex and beautiful being.

At first sight one is not sure if she is to be a friend or foe. Some of the trainees were also unsure. On the first night I recall chatting to a very upset trainee who was both seasick and homesick. I suggested that by the end of the voyage she would be having so much fun she would not want to leave. On prizegiving night this youngster won the award for having got the most from the voyage.

Our voyage took in the rugged east coastline of the South Island, including the remote and very beautiful Stewart Island. Dolphins, seals and all manner of bird life (particularly 'shags' whose name for some reason provided no end of entertainment) accompanied us on our voyage. The lack of wind meant there was very little sailing to be done, but lessons were still learnt — though not always about how to flake a rope, rig the frapping straps or set the topgallant sail.

Once on board, the first big challenge all trainees faced was 'going aloft'. Basically this means scampering skywards to a very high and, for many, terrifying place. Safety is the biggest issue on the ship though, and everyone wears a safety harness at all times when above deck.

Before this voyage I had believed I was the only one suffering from a fear of heights. This was not true. On the second day when I assisted the trainees over the futtock for their first climb, I noticed most were afraid and some shook even more than I had! It was very comforting to know that I was not alone in this fear and also to realise the power gained in facing that fear head-on in a safe and supported environment. *Spirit* teaches us to push the traditional boundaries we set for ourselves.

The daily 6am icy cold swim off the side of the boat was another lesson in dealing with fears. This was a rude awakening to be sure, but a most practical way of conserving water, cleaning all on board and fully waking everyone for a day packed with activity. Trainees who struggled with this on day one were waterbabies by the end of the voyage.

The high ropes course that we climbed in Akaroa Harbour provided a third

A HUMAN TOPSAIL

On one occasion, the topsail was torn early in the voyage and had been sent back to Auckland for repair. The lack of this important sail was evident to all, and towards the end of the trip, my watch of girls, of their own volition and with permission, climbed the mast and stood on the foot rope of the top mast yard as a makeshift topsail. Not as efficient as the real thing, but it certainly made a difference. I was very proud of those girls.
BRUCE LETHBRIDGE
Volunteer crew

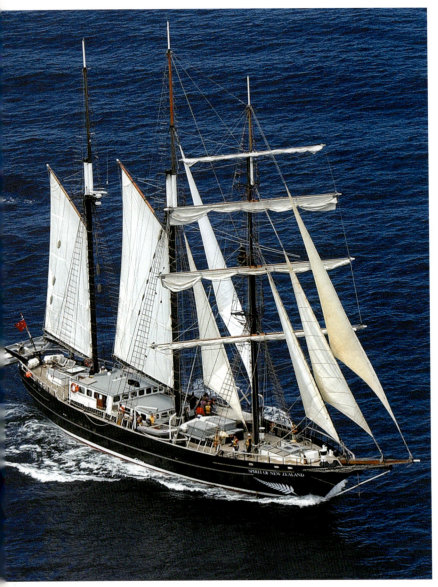

Spirit of New Zealand in Bluff Harbour, weekend voyage 384SP to Stewart Island, November 2002.

(Peter Meecham, *The Southland Times*)

major challenge. For this course, ropes were rigged from mast to mast in all manners possible and harnesses were donned by each trainee. My legs have never shaken so much as when I dangled between the masts, gripping one rope with my hands and another with my feet, many metres above the deck.

One trainee in my watch initially refused to participate in this course. She was terrified and believed she couldn't do it. By the end of the day, with support from her watch and encouragement from the crew, she had completed both courses. The smile on her face was enormous. This day was really about people working together, supporting one another and conquering fears. It was also about mental strength, and saying 'I can do this'.

The crew were a slightly mad bunch, but in the best of ways. If safety was the biggest issue on board, having fun followed a close second. I laughed more during those ten days than I had in years, often to the point of tears. I am convinced that people go slightly mad at sea. Sleep deprivation may contribute to this.

Spirit nurtures an environment where the trainees (and crew) can be who they want to be. There are no rules about this, and it was a delight to watch the process unfold and old patterns disappear. There was one trainee on board who didn't smile until day seven, and when he laughed on day eight I knew the *Spirit* magic was working! For me this was the best moment of the voyage.

No two trainees are from the same school, so 40 strangers have the opportunity to come on board and be exactly who they want to be for ten days. Stephanie Bristol from the Trust's operations office says, 'The only thing anyone knows about the trainees' backgrounds is what they choose to share.' Hence *Spirit of New Zealand* is about young people having the opportunity for a clean slate, to break the mould of their circumstances and the ideas they have held about themselves — to be the person they want to be.

Every day, time was devoted to teamwork and confidence building. Everything is geared towards the last day, 'Trainee Day', when the trainees have full rein to sail the vessel. Problem-solving skills, planning and the ability to work together as a team are paramount on this day.

At the start of my voyage it baffled me just how this group of young, mainly inexperienced trainees would be able to sail and navigate this complex vessel on Trainee Day after just nine days together. But it happened! The process was incredible, not as a lesson in sailing, but as a lesson in life.

It works like this. Each *Spirit* voyage is divided into three phases and each phase lasts for three days. Phase one is 'hands on', when the crew show the trainees how to sail the boat. Phase two is 'hands on over their hands', when the trainees are monitored and the crew and trainees work together to sail the vessel. Phase three or 'hands free' is when the trainees are largely responsible for the sailing and the role of the crew is to help if needed and to 'see the results and praise the achievement'. On the final day the trainees were chomping at the bit to sail *Spirit* themselves, and sail her they did — arriving at their destination only minutes before the deadline.

Every day each 'watch' would work together, first on their cleaning duties and later on their sail station. The role of leader always rotated. This allowed the most

A group photo is taken every voyage. This is Voyage 357, *Spirit of New Zealand*.

unexpected leaders to 'come out' and shine. The quietest trainees often made the most wonderful leaders. This was proved on Trainee Day when the individual voted as 'captain' for the day was in fact a quietly spoken lass with superb leadership qualities.

The ten days spent on board *Spirit* were some of the most intense, difficult and rewarding of my life. I thought a great deal, particularly about how the power of the mind can define our actions and dictate who we are and how we relate to the world around us.

Spirit teaches young people (and old fogies like me) to feel the fear and do it anyway. She teaches the quietest and most humble individuals that there is power and leadership within and that we can be who we want to be. *Spirit* is neither a friend nor foe. She is a wise old soul and she is exactly who we make her.

A LIFE-CHANGING EXPERIENCE

RUTH DOBSON-SMITH

Ruth Dobson-Smith sailed as a trainee on Spirit of New Zealand *Voyage 271 in September 1998. She has since crewed as leading hand and has been a regular member of the volunteer crew. Following her trainee voyage, Ruth joined the Canterbury branch of the Voyagers Club where she served as membership coordinator and as president from 1998 to 2000. She was rosterer in 1999-2000 on the Voyagers Club National Executive. Ruth now lives in Dunedin where she is studying for her BTchg (Primary) and BA (Music and English) degrees.*

As a trainee on Voyage 140 (Auckland to Auckland) I had some of the best experiences of my life so far.

I would like to thank everyone on board, especially those people who helped guide us through our ten days aboard. I grew to admire all of the people aboard in control of us because of the way they competently instilled in us the confidence in our own ability that enabled us to take control of the ship for a day.

Since my voyage away I have had a successful year in terms of schooling and private achievements. I feel that a lot of my achievements can be attributed to the sail-training scheme for giving me the confidence in myself that I needed to succeed. Thank you for a wonderful experience!! (Abridged)

ADAM LOVELL
Trainee, Voyage 140
(*Spirit of New Zealand,* 1993)

MY FIFTH FORM year at Christchurch Girls' High School gave me the opportunity to participate on Voyage 271 on *Spirit of New Zealand*. This ten-day youth development voyage motivated me and brought out things inside me that no other experience could. It changed me for life.

As I was a thoroughly organised 15-year-old, I quickly learnt about the Trust. I went to the public library to read books about *Spirit* and treated any correspondence between me and the Trust as gold. My anticipation and excitement levels grew daily. Fundraising was an ordeal I put my heart and soul into, asking donations from local Lions and Rotary clubs as well as the Christchurch Community Trust. All requests were fulfilled with great generosity and I was very grateful for this funding.

Finally September rolled round. It was time to take the adventure that has contributed so greatly to my personal identity today. I wanted to make the most of the opportunity. I was very confident but I was young, and travelling the distance from Christchurch to Auckland was a challenge. Only half a dozen of us on the voyage came from south of Christchurch, and these people became my best friends. We were forced into a confined space on the bus and ferry for 20 hours of 'getting to know each other'. The ability to get on with other people is a skill needed in so many life experiences and one which I have had to use frequently in my association with *Spirit*.

The trip itself was amazing. It's a cheesy expression, but words simply cannot express what it was like. Even now, if I meet someone new and find that they have been on *Spirit*, conversation suddenly becomes easy. *Spirit* has that spark that unites young New Zealanders all over the country. The ten days were filled to the brim with learning sails, nautical laws, 6am swims, walks ashore... It was endless and tiring fun. I have so many memories that I have shared with so many people. But what meant most to me, what changed me for life, was the people — the crew, the trainees and especially the Voyagers later on.

On board I learnt numerous skills which I still refer to and use in day-to-day activities. I had very successful sixth and seventh form years (including a 'service to school award') and then left the comforting world of Christchurch to embark on another life adventure at Otago University. Five years of hard-core learning will push me out into the bigger and scarier workforce. And I couldn't have got to where I am now without the essential skills of leadership, communication and confidence I achieved on Voyage 271.

I don't think I could have gained these skills alone. The 'people' made it happen. I recall my first time climbing the rigging up to the royal sail. I was scared, and it showed. Sweat pouring down my face, hands and legs shaking... I was a mess. But I had to achieve this task. It took leadership, communication and confidence. I wanted to prove to my team that anything could be achieved, and it was. My team talked me through it, pushed me to my extreme limits. It was a very satisfying experience.

I walked off that boat, my boat, a changed person. Everyone did. Little did I know that there was a lot more of the *Spirit* experience to come. I returned to Christchurch determined to stay lifelong friends with these people. Some I am still very close to and I have met many others along the way. I was invited into the Canterbury Voyagers Club and given a great welcome. Everyone claimed that I still had the 'boat buzz' and that my enthusiasm was a great asset to the club. I became an active member and worked hard at growing its numbers. The Voyagers conference at Easter developed the skills originally learnt and explored on *Spirit* on my ten-day voyage. I met friends from all over the country, friends who have supported me continuously. I don't know what I'd do without them. Thanks guys!

Now, as I continue my life studies, not a day goes by without my thinking about what I gained from *Spirit*. I will continue my involvement with the Trust, working towards helping more and more young New Zealanders change their lives for the better. Just as *Spirit* changed mine.

I continue to be impressed by the friendly, caring, professional approach demonstrated by staff at the operations office. Dealing with 400 schools and a myriad of youth and service groups must not be easy. In every trainee application there is an expectant or anxious youngster and at least one equally anxious parent, who together wonder about the efficiency and accountability of the operation, the safety, the practicalities of travel and of establishing contact — particularly for the small-town student required to arrive at Queen's Wharf. I do not receive adverse comments from parents or trainees. I do receive satisfaction, thanks, expressions of pride and a clear impression that little could be improved. I read of our trainees, particularly girls, sustaining their interest and commitment by assuming roles in the [Voyagers] Club — surely this is demonstrating leadership and a desire to do for others what they have experienced: in short, true citizenship.

Let's be honest. It is hard to measure the lasting benefits of a ten-day voyage on a young person. Perhaps I am in a privileged position. I can ask a question of a student and get an immediate, positive response, with eye-to-eye affirmation: 'That voyage was very important to me.'

Young New Zealanders need the opportunity for a sustained challenge — a challenge that is affordable to many and, with subsidy or sponsorship, available to most if not all teenagers — a challenge that is proven. The Spirit of Adventure Trust is unique in New Zealand. Its challenge is our challenge for tomorrow.

(Abridged)

G INNES
Divisional Principal
Burnside High School, Christchurch, 1993

ULTIMATE CHALLENGE

GEORGE BRIGHTWELL

George Brightwell of Opaheke High School sailed on Spirit of New Zealand, *Voyage 320, in 2000.*

BLOOD PUMPS furiously through my veins, which bulge on my fevered brow. Anxiety tears at my chest as I glimpse the looming mast, a dark fixture towering above the rest of the boat – an obstacle, an adversary I must challenge to topple my growing fear of heights. My strong heart, now turning to mush, is still pounding vigorously as I raise my head to have another look.

Looking up, I know I don't want to attempt the challenge, but a constant nagging feeling keeps me on my toes. First, we put on our yellows (wet weather gear) and strap ourselves tightly into a safety harness. Slowly, I make my way over to the mast, listening to the steady swish, swish, swish of the lapping waves hitting the side of the ship.

It is unbelievably high! Seventy foot plus! Fear begins to seep silently from my subconscious, threatening to strike my fragile mind. My fellow trainees are eager to climb, giving me encouragement. I step out and around the ladder, placing my foot on the first rung. The ladder has black metal rungs criss-crossing with wooden rungs. We were carefully instructed to step on the wooden ones and grab the metal ones as we climb. I take a deep breath and try to raise my arm, but to my astonishment, it won't move. My feet suddenly are like cement super-glued to the railing. My body is an ice cube refusing to budge!

'Keep a move on,' comes the fiery command of our captain, thawing my frozen body and mind, making me active again. I glance out to sea, take another deep breath and begin my trek up the mast. Keep going, keep going, keep going, I tell myself. I look out. The sea expands for miles, vast and mysterious. The outline of the North Island looks ghostly in the hovering mist. Dark grey clouds lumber above us, threatening rain. The wild westerly wind whips my face. The bitter salt taste that floats with it attacks my tastebuds. The number one rule, we are told, is not to look down. But I do. I look down.

My stomach suddenly leaps up and I only just catch it in my mouth. I lurch forward, letting one hand off the railing. I swing out. Half my body dangles in mid-air. My head spins. Am I going to fall? My mind is reeling; I struggle to constrain my imagination. Is this how it is going to end? A sharp pain shoots across my shoulder. A strong vice-like grip brings me back to reality. A calm voice echoes in my ear, settling my nerves. My blurry vision begins to focus properly. A shocking realisation hits me hard. Both my hands are still on the railing!

'You OK, man?' someone enquires.

'I'm all right,' I mutter, regaining my composure.

'You sort of froze for a minute.'

'I'm all right!' I reply aggressively, not wanting any of his sympathy.

A rough push on my leg tells me I'd better get a move on. Shaking off my worries, I recommence my climb. Sweat pours down my face like a free-flowing river. My breaths come out in short gasps, chest heaving. Still, I am getting higher and higher. My adrenalin level is at its maximum, my excited body is pumped as I'm now looking forward to the challenge of reaching the top. Power surges through my muscles. The tip of the mast grows bigger. I'm nearly there! My muscles complain as I exceed my limits. Agony has found a home. Two more rungs to go. I reach out, stretching my arm, gripping the very tip of the mast. I've done it! I have achieved the impossible! I am at the very top! I can see everything! I'm lost for words. Happiness floods through my body. I am at peace.

'Right then.' A voice interrupts my moment of joy. 'Time to go down.' Down! I could barely get up!

NURTURING LEADERSHIP

BRONWYN RHYND

Bronwyn Rhynd was a trainee on Spirit of Adventure *in 1980. Following her voyage she joined the Whangarei branch of the Voyagers Club and became president of the club's national executive in 1985. Bronwyn is an environmental engineer and lives in Auckland.*

MY INVOLVEMENT and experiences with the Spirit of Adventure Trust and both ships have been as a trainee, voyage leader and Voyager. This has led to various adventures and experiences that have and will continue to have an impact on my life.

As a trainee I was a very young and naive country girl following in my elder sister's footsteps. I always admired and envied my sister, so I embraced the opportunity to enter the *Spirit* world with great enthusiasm. I had a wonderful trip on *Spirit of Adventure* along with the other trainees. We had loads of laughter and moments of terror as we ventured into the nautical world with no experience but a bundle of enthusiasm. On that trip we visited *Esmeralda*, the Chilean naval sail-training ship. I guess the crew could hardly believe their eyes when 20 female trainees boarded the ship as guests!

The natural progression was to return to *Spirit* as a voyage leader (now 'leading hand'), the go-between between trainees and crew. This gave me another chance to experience tall ship sailing. My time as a trainee had only whetted my appetite! By this stage I had joined the Voyagers Club and got to know a few crew members personally, so this voyage was very enjoyable from the moment we left the wharf. It was also a chance for me to reflect on my trainee experience, a rare opportunity at a young age to see the progress I was making in my life. My time as a voyage leader was my first real role of responsibility outside my work environment.

The voyage leader experience clinched my desire to be involved in the whole Spirit organisation and led me to become very involved in the Voyagers Club. It also gave me instant friendships when I was away from home and in a new city with no close support network.

From being a local representative in the Whangarei branch of the Voyagers Club to taking on the role of president of the national executive of the Voyagers Club, I was given opportunities that other New Zealanders would be unlikely to be presented with at similar stages of their lives.

Undoubtedly the opportunities were there, because the Spirit organisation is a vehicle for nurturing leadership qualities. During my time with the Voyagers I was lucky enough to speak for the youth of New Zealand by representing the Voyagers

Having been a [trainee] on Spirit of New Zealand *Voyage 101 in December 1990 and found I thoroughly enjoyed the experience, I would very much like to go back as a leading hand.*

Spirit of New Zealand *gave me new growth and an experience I'll never forget. Working as a team, trusting one another and relying on one another made me feel like a worthwhile person.* Spirit *brought out leadership skills which I thought I never had.*

Going back on Spirit *would boost my confidence even more. I feel that showing others what I've learnt will teach me new skills, and will also once again enable me to feel part of something special and to acquire more good memories!*

(Abridged)

HAMISH GOLDSACK

Trainee, Voyage 101, 1990

Scrubbing the decks!

Club at the Spirit of Adventure Trust Board meetings. This was very daunting at first, knowing that there were some very experienced and highly influential people sitting on the Trust Board. I would travel down from Whangarei in my very old, noisy car and park in a very fancy building, trying to hide it next to its European counterparts. I'm sure this was much to the amusement of the tenants of the building, and they didn't miss that car once I managed to change to a quieter (but alas not European) model.

As president of the club I would organise like-minded souls to support the Spirit organisation in various ways. However, our activities of course had a youthful slant. Annually we would gather for a conference, usually in a remote and also very cold part of New Zealand. (Why was it always in winter?) Anyway, half of the conference experience was the travel. From the top to the bottom of the country, various means of transport would bring the Voyagers Club members together. A weekend of fun, mischief and of course the AGM.

Another memorable experience was representing the Spirit organisation during the launch of *Spirit of New Zealand* by speaking at a function in the aft cabin in the presence of Prince Philip. I was very honoured to be asked and overwhelmed with the protocol that this occasion involved. The information arriving by post from the Department of Internal Affairs was enough to give me butterflies in my stomach. It also made me realise that I was a leader within a group of New Zealand youth. Until then the path I had taken was not really a conscious one, more one that 'happened along the way'. The task of writing a speech to be heard by a varied audience including royalty was difficult, but with a little help from other Spirit friends the end result was delivered to a very responsive audience. I must admit my nerves at that function were only calmed with the sherry we drank at the end.

Soon after the royal experience, my involvement with the Voyagers Club came to an end as I took on another challenge, joining the Operation Raleigh expedition and heading off to Chile. Whether my experiences with the Spirit organisation helped my selection for the Operation Raleigh expedition I don't know. All I do know is that they certainly gave me the courage to put myself forward for selection and the skills to organise people to take the best advantage of their combined abilities.

LASTING MEMORIES

CATHERINE WOODWARD

Catherine Woodward (née Garrett) was a trainee on Voyage 11, the first all-girls' voyage on Spirit of Adventure *in June 1974. She now lives in Canberra, Australia.*

WHEN *SPIRIT OF ADVENTURE* was commissioned I can remember thinking, 'I want to sail on that ship'. So, when I was chosen to represent Westlake Girls High School on the first all-girls' crew, I was rapt. It was winter 1974, and we sailed with a crew made up of 30 girls. Our captain was Pony More, the mate Ron Bird and our female watch leader, Helen Partridge. The voyage was the most intense ten days I have ever spent. It was absolutely wonderful.

The best part of the trip was crossing from Kawau Island to the Coromandel Peninsula in 50-plus-knot winds. We had the lee rail under the water with very little sail up. The weather was freezing cold. My best memory is sitting out on the bowsprit on that leg with a friend in our wet weather gear. It was unreal.

Because it was the first girls' voyage, there was more publicity for the trip than was usual. The first day, while we were waiting for some of the girls to arrive, the *New Zealand Women's Weekly* interviewed and photographed us. I remember seeing the published article. Near the end of the trip, we sailed up the harbour in light winds with as much sail as we could carry. The square sails had not been delivered yet, but the cross spars were in place. Eight of us climbed up the rigging and out along the cross spars. There was a photo of us in *The New Zealand Herald* the next day.

The voyage on *Spirit of Adventure* is one of the highlights of my life. It was a wonderful opportunity for an academically-minded teenager to experience something completely different — a real adventure.

HEIDI MILLER

Heidi Miller was a trainee on Voyage 260 in May 1998. She comes from Nelson.

THE WIND IS 25 knots and the ship is plunging up and down, up and down in the huge swell. It is so rough that even some of the crew are ill. We feel nearly dead. What are we doing on this stupid ship anyway? Well, we are supposed to be having a glorious time, the experience of a lifetime, on a beautiful black sailing ship called *Spirit of New Zealand*.

But here we are, leaning on the rails, vomiting and heaving over the side with others lying on the deck in various shades of green, looking like death warmed up. We are all harnessed on to the side so we don't fall overboard — but we wouldn't

Two current masters: Nigel Wright (left) (Susanna Burton) **and Jim Dilley.**

care if we did. There are different colours and lumps of vomit on the rim all around the sides of the boat and even on the deck.

A few awful people with cast-iron stomachs are laughing and eating their tea quite happily, while the rest of us unfortunates retch and vomit again and again. Who could even look at stew and custard? This is my idea of hell.

Down under the deck in our cabin it is even worse. Our sleeping area is so small that we have to walk sideways to get past each other and the beds are just too narrow to be even remotely comfortable. Twenty-one girl trainees are cramped into this crowded sleeping area. With each wave we are flung across the room, against the walls or each other. We take turns at kneeling on the floor and spewing into the toilets and plastic cleaning buckets. How I am going to get into my tiny bunk, in the third tier up against the ceiling, I honestly don't know. The smell and heat in the bunk room is enough to make anyone sick.

Each of us silently endures our misery, and the boys are just as bad as the girls. Nine more days of this and I think I will be dead. We look through the porthole and see sky, and next thing the porthole is under water. People who have been on this boat and told me the trip would be marvellous need their heads read.

It will be good to go home, but now we don't really want to leave the ship. It will be sad saying goodbye to all our mates. We have had such a good time (after the first few days of hideous seasickness). We have done so many things together: tying knots, learning navigation, climbing the mast, doing night watch. Having a close look at steaming White Island, photographing dolphins, the water fight when the captain jumped overboard in his clothes. We had fun with the egg competition, dropping an egg from the mast and trying not to break it! Those awful 6am swims that made us feel so good afterwards. Rowing in the rubber duckies in the dark with phosphorus glowing green in the water around us. Walking on the squeaky white sand of Sir Michael Fay's hideaway Great Mercury Island. Tramping through the bush on Great Barrier Island: the famous four-hour tramp that turned out to be six and a half hours and covered miles and miles! Our excitement as we sailed under the Auckland Harbour Bridge.

After berthing in Auckland, I bought a souvenir jacket that will last me for years. On the sleeve it says 'Skippered it, scaled it, steered it, sailed it, scrubbed it, survived it!'

And we did.

GLOSSARY

Note: Many of the words included in this glossary are capable of several definitions. The definitions given below relate specifically to the context in which the words are used in this book.

Aft At or towards the stern (back) of a ship.

Backstay A stay (q.v.) which supports a mast from astern (behind).

Barque A sailing ship with at least three and up to five masts. All masts except the aftermast (rear mast) are square-rigged. The aftermast is rigged fore-and-aft.

Barquentine A sailing ship with three or more masts. The foremast (front mast) is square-rigged. All other masts are rigged fore-and-aft.

Boom A horizontal pole attached to the mast and to which the foot of the sail is fastened.

Bowsprit A spar which projects from the bow of a sailing ship and is used to provide an attachment for the forestays and carry the headstay and headsails.

Brace A rope attached to the ends of each yard and used to pivot the yards around the mast to allow square sails to catch the wind.

Brigantine A sailing ship with two masts. The foremast (front mast) is rigged square and the mainmast rigged fore-and-aft.

Buntline A line fastened to the foot of a square sail and used to haul the sail up to the yard when furling.

Capstan A device sometimes used for heaving on heavy ropes.

Clew The two bottom corners of a square sail or the after (back) lower corner of a fore-and-aft sail.

Clewline A rope used to haul up the clew of a square sail when furling it.

Close-hauled Sailing with the wind coming from an angle ahead of the vessel.

Course sail The lowest square sail, set from the ship's lowest yard.

Dory A rowing boat, sometimes used as a ship's boat.

Foot The lower edge of a sail.

Fore At or toward a ship's bow (front).

Forestay A stay (q.v.) supporting a mast from ahead (in front).

Furl To roll up and secure a sail to a yard or boom.

Futtock shrouds Short shrouds (q.v.) above the main shrouds and below a top (q.v.) which help to support a mast.

Gaff A spar to which the head of a fore-and-aft sail is attached.

Gaff-rigged Rigged with one or more gaff sails.

Gaff sail A four-sided fore-and-aft sail.

Gybe When the wind is coming from astern (behind), a controlled action which transfers a fore-and-aft sail from one side of the ship to the other. (An uncontrolled gybe can be dangerous.)

Hawser A heavy rope for mooring or towing.

Head The upper corner of a triangular sail or the upper side of a gaff sail.

Headsail A general term for sails set forward of the foremast.

Jib boom The spar (q.v.) extending the bowsprit and to which the upper forestays are secured.

Ketch A two-masted fore-and-aft rigged vessel with a taller mainmast and a shorter mizzenmast (q.v.).

Lee The side away from the direction from which the wind is blowing.

Mizzenmast The aftermast (rear mast).

Raffee A triangular sail set from the foremast head above the square topsail (*Spirit of Adventure*).

Ratlines A series of light rope or wooden steps secured across the shrouds of a sailing ship, forming a ladder for climbing aloft.

Reaching Sailing with the wind coming from abeam (right angles) or at an angle astern of (behind) the vessel.

Royal sail The uppermost square sail on the foremast (*Spirit of New Zealand*).

Running Sailing with the wind coming from astern (behind) or nearly astern of the vessel.

Schooner A fore-and-aft rigged sailing vessel with at least two masts. The masts may be of equal height or the foremast may be the shorter of the two. A topsail schooner carries one or more square topsails.

Shackle A U-shaped bracket, closed with a pin, used for securing ropes.

Shrouds The wires supporting the masts and secured at the vessel's sides.

Spar A general term for a wooden pole to which sails are attached.

Square-rigger A sailing ship rigged with rectangular sails set on horizontal yards at right angles to the keel.

Square sails The rectangular sails of a square rigger. On *Spirit of New Zealand*, the four square sails are (from top) the royal, topgallant, topsail and course. On *Spirit of Adventure*, the three foremast sails were (from top) the raffee (triangular), topsail and course.

Stay A wire (usually one of a set) used for supporting a mast.

Staysail A sail hoisted up on a stay.

Tack A course sailed by a sailing vessel. When the wind is coming from ahead (in front), a manoeuvre to alter course which transfers a fore-and-aft sail from one side of the ship to another.

Top A platform at the head of a mast section used primarily to spread the shrouds.

Topgallant A square sail set immediately above the square topsail.

Topsail A square sail set immediately above the course sail or a triangular sail above a gaff.

Windlass Deck machinery used primarily to raise and lower the anchor.

Yard A length of rounded timber (a spar, q.v.) secured at right angles to the mast from which square sails are set.

Yardarms The two tapering outer ends of a ship's yard.

APPENDIX 1

WINNERS OF TOPSAIL AWARDS

The Spirit of Adventure Trust Board presents these awards for outstanding contributions to the Voyagers Club and for supporting the sail-training principles of the Spirit of Adventure Trust Board.

2001 (INAUGURAL YEAR)
Brian Orr (Auckland)
Brenda Boekhorst (Auckland)
Helen Takacs (Wellington)

2002
Andrea Tomlinson (Nelson)
2003
Veronica Gailitis (Wellington)

APPENDIX 2

WINNERS OF TOPGALLANT AWARDS

The Topgallant Award acknowledges members who have contributed more than ten years' outstanding service to the Spirit of Adventure Trust Board.

1998 (INAUGURAL YEAR)
Ron Blackman (Auckland) for services as volunteer crew.
Ron Bird (Auckland) for services as engineer, volunteer crew and archivist.
Alan Crabbe (Napier) for services as port contact for Napier and volunteer crew.
Roy Freeland (Dunedin) (posthumously) for services as port contact for Dunedin and volunteer crew.
Jim Frew (Auckland) for services as advisory medical officer and volunteer crew.
Nick Hylton (Auckland) for services as master and for developing the basis of the Trust's education programme.
Paul Leppington (Auckland) for services as master, rigger and advocate for sail training.
Peter and Rona McConachy (Whangarei) for services as port contacts for Northland and volunteer crew.
Bruce Marler (Auckland) for services as founding trustee and volunteer crew.
Colin Shields (Wellington) for services to the Wellington Regional Association.
Adrienne Welch (Auckland) for services as Voyagers Club coordinator, port contact for Wellington and volunteer crew.

1999
Barry Thompson (Auckland) for services as founding trustee and volunteer crew.
Joyce Lavender QSO (Wellington) for services to the Trust through her involvement with young persons with disabilities.

2000
Ivor Sanders (Wellington) for services as port contact for Wellington, as volunteer crew and to the Wellington Regional Association.
Tom Sawyer (Southland) for services as volunteer master.
2001
Tim Ridge (Auckland) for services as a permanent and volunteer master.
John Reeves (Motueka) for services as a permanent and volunteer mate.
2002
Simon Carryer (Auckland) for services as the Auckland Regional Association chairperson, rosterer and volunteer mate.
Pierce Prendergast (Christchurch) for services as port contact for Christchurch.
2003
Jim Varney (Auckland) for services as a long-serving trustee, deputy chairman and volunteer master.
Jane Bethell (Auckland) for services as a founding member of the national Voyagers Club, to the Auckland Regional Association and as volunteer crew.

APPENDIX 3

TRUSTEES OF THE SPIRIT OF ADVENTURE TRUST

CURRENT TRUSTEES

	TRUSTEE DATE OF APPOINTMENT
Stephen Fisher (founding trustee)	February 1973 (chairman since September 1977)
John Duder	December 1976
John King	July 1989 (deputy chairman since October 2002)
Tessa Duder	November 1992
Captain Ron McKenzie	October 1998
Anthony Frankham	May 1999
Mike Hutcheson	February 2002
Captain Mike Austin	February 2003
Margaret Bendall	July 2003

FORMER TRUSTEES

	TRUSTEE DATE OF APPOINTMENT
Lou Fisher (founding trustee and chairman)	February 1973
Captain Barry Thompson (founding trustee)	February 1973 (appointed deputy chairman in June 1992)
John McKenzie (founding trustee)	February 1973 (appointed deputy chairman in August 1978)
Rear-Admiral Laurie Carr (founding trustee and deputy chairman)	February 1973
Simon Caughey (founding trustee)	February 1973
Peter Mulgrew (founding trustee)	February 1973
John Brooke (founding trustee)	February 1973
Dr Colin Maiden (founding trustee)	February 1973
Bruce Marler	March 1974 (appointed deputy chairman in 1989)
James Lennox-King	October 1974
Noel Robinson	October 1975
Tim Savage	October 1975
Bill Craike	July 1976
Penny Whiting	April 1980
Captain Jim Varney	April 1980 (appointed deputy chairman in July 1998)
Captain Fred Huddleston	April 1980
Frank Innes-Jones	September 1981
Admiral Sir Gordon Tait	July 1982
Ann Gluckman	July 1989
Gill Hubble	February 1996
Roy Swan	July 1997
Sylvie Wilkinson	March 2000

APPENDIX 4

MASTERS OF *SPIRIT OF ADVENTURE* AND *SPIRIT OF NEW ZEALAND*

Since its inception in 1973, the Spirit of Adventure Trust has benefited from the services of a large number of experienced permanent, relieving and volunteer masters. These masters are listed below in approximate order of their first involvement with the Trust.

PERMANENT OR CONTRACT RELIEVING MASTERS

Pony More
Glen Cornthwaite
Keith Paxman
Stan Hulford
Colin Quincey
Jack Habberfield
Fred Hansen
Alan Wallis
Peter van der Sloot
Jim Revell
Nick Hylton
Gordon Ingram
Peter Petherbridge
Jennifer Roberts
Paul Leppington
Ken Bedford
Alan Wilson
Margaret Pidgeon
Ian Rankin
Tom Sawyer
Bill Curry
Steve Gamble
Nigel Wright
Lisa Romero
Jim Dilley
Paul Dukes
Neil Rowarth
Mike Foster
Jim Lott
Gordon Hayward

VOLUNTEER OR OCCASIONAL RELIEVING MASTERS

J Littler
Barry Thompson
Mel Bowen
Jim Varney
Con Thode
Brian Whiteman
Mike Austin
Roy Swann
Tim Ridge
Geoff Rowarth
Rick Hunter
Murray Lister
Lew Henderson
Ian Webb
Ken Marshall
Jan Rowden
Andrew Lidguard